EACH MOMENT IS THE UNIVERSE

OTHER BOOKS BY DAININ KATAGIRI ROSHI

Returning to Silence: Zen Practice in Daily Life

You Have to Say Something: Manifesting Zen Insight

EACH MOMENT IS THE UNIVERSE

Zen and the Way of Being Time

DAININ KATAGIRI

Edited by Andrea Martin

SHAMBHALA

Boston & London

2007

SHAMBHALA PUBLICATIONS, INC.

Horticultural Hall
300 Massachusetts Avenue
Boston, Massachusetts 02115
www.shambhala.com

9 8 7 6 5 4 3 2 1
First Edition
Printed in the United States of America

⊗ This edition is printed on acid-free paper that meets the American
National Standards Institute z39.48 Standard.

Distributed in the United States by Random House, Inc., and in
Canada by Random House of Canada Ltd

Designed by Barbara Jellow

Library of Congress Cataloging-in-Publication Data

Katagiri, Dainin, 1928–
Each moment is the universe: Zen and the way of being time /
Dainin Katagiri; edited by Andrea Martin.
p. cm.
Includes bibliographical references and index.
ISBN 978-1-59030-408-2 (alk. paper)
1. Time—Religious aspects—Zen Buddhism. 2. Zen Buddhism—
Doctrines. 3. Sotoshu—Doctrines. I. Martin, Andrea, 1948– II. Title.

BQ9268.6.K38 2007
294.3'420427—DC22
2006102968

CONTENTS

EDITOR'S PREFACE

Katagiri Roshi had a profoundly positive view of life. He taught that reality is beautiful and the scale of our lives is larger than we can imagine. He tirelessly explained Buddhism, taught how to study and practice Zen, and encouraged people to continue their quest for a peaceful life.

Time was a central element in the teachings of Katagiri Roshi. He used time as a unifying theme to explain the Buddhist way of life and to encourage wholehearted spiritual practice. The study of time typically belongs to the world of philosophy, physics, or cosmology. So it may be surprising to see this book on time according to Zen Buddhism. Yet insight into the nature of time is a key to understanding Zen.

What does Zen Buddhism say about time? We usually think of time as something that is separate from us. We measure time as a commodity or a resource and use it to shape our lives. Then we judge and evaluate ourselves according to how we save, spend, make, buy, use, or waste time. When time is separate from us, it may become an opponent in the game of life. Then we're in a race to beat the clock, hoping that at the end of the day we'll be a winner. In Buddhism, however, time is more than this.

Katagiri Roshi explained time as a dynamic activity that is integrated with life, not separate from life.

In this book, the word time is used in more than one way. In some cases it refers to our usual idea of time, and in others it has a deeper meaning. In presenting the total picture of time, Katagiri Roshi said it is important to study time intellectually because it helps us to understand the reality of the world we live in and to see the meaning of Buddhist philosophy. Yet to fully understand time we need a spiritual practice as well. Katagiri Roshi taught that Zen meditation is a way to discover the true nature of human life and to experience what time is by becoming one with its dynamic activity.

When he died, Katagiri Roshi left as part of his legacy a large audio archive of recorded talks. The teachings in this book come from that archive and are taken from talks he gave at various times over his last twenty years. Some of the talks were given in the intense environment of a meditation retreat, others were offered to a more general audience.

To create this book, I selected talks in which time played an important role and arranged them according to the structure of the Four Noble Truths. The doctrine of the Four Noble Truths was the first teaching of the historical Buddha, in which he explained that dissatisfaction and suffering are inherent in human life and described a path of action that takes human experience beyond dissatisfaction and suffering to joy.

Part 1 looks at time itself, with an emphasis on impermanence. Part 2 introduces the first two Noble Truths:

suffering is inherent in human life, and there is a cause of suffering. Part 3 reflects the third truth: there is freedom from suffering. Part 4 is inspired by the fourth truth: there is a path of action in which freedom relieves suffering. Part 5 investigates karma, a complicated topic that is usually studied with the second truth but is presented separately here within the context of Buddhism's positive view of life and hope for the future. In the final chapter, these strands come together in one expression of Buddha's teaching. It is not necessary to read the book in this order, because the division of ideas is not as tidy as this overview implies, but it might be more satisfying, because many of the ideas develop as the book unfolds.

Katagiri Roshi's talks were thoroughly oral teachings. He planned in advance yet spoke spontaneously. Sometimes he jumped to new ideas or circled back to earlier ones. Talks could be repetitious, giving people more than one opportunity to hear the points he was making. To coax from these talks the structure required by the printed page, I reorganized them and made them more concise. To maintain the narrative flow of the book, I took some talks apart and combined them with others so that ideas came together. I edited Katagiri Roshi's words to smooth out his expression but preserved his manner of speaking and vocabulary, always listening to hear his voice through the words.

Some of Katagiri Roshi's teachings were quite challenging and complex. In editing his talks, I have done my best to represent his ideas accurately and at the same time make them readily understandable. For any errors I have made in presenting his meaning, I humbly offer my apology.

I met and began to study with Katagiri Roshi at the Minnesota Zen Meditation Center in 1978. In the beginning it was difficult to grasp the meaning of his teaching, but his presence manifested something that compelled me to continue. Eventually we had many discussions about Zen, and I was fortunate to serve as his attendant on many occasions and also as his secretary toward the end of his life. I remain filled with gratitude for his efforts to show me the true nature of my life and for his support of my spiritual journey.

Katagiri Roshi's manifestation of the Buddha Way touched the hearts of many people. Although he died in 1990, he is widely remembered and appreciated today. I hope that those who knew him, those who have studied his teachings, and those who are discovering him now will have a sense of meeting Katagiri Roshi in this book.

Andrea Martin

ACKNOWLEDGMENTS

A substantial portion of part 1 is taken from talks that Katagiri Roshi gave at San Francisco Zen Center before he began teaching in Minnesota. Thank you to San Francisco Zen Center for creating transcripts of these talks and giving me permission to use them.

In part 3 Katagiri Roshi presents a partial translation of Dogen's *Shobogenzo,* "Being-Time." This translation was made by Katagiri Roshi based on a translation made by Kazuaki Tanahashi and Dan Welch at the San Francisco Zen Center. Their translation later appeared in the book *Moon in a Dewdrop.* Thank you to the translators and to San Francisco Zen Center for permission to use their work here.

Many people deserve to be acknowledged and appreciated for their contributions to the creation of this book. Thank you to Rev. Karen Sunna, who, when she was abbot of Minnesota Zen Meditation Center, was immediately supportive of my idea for the book, and to Rev. Tim Burkett, our current abbot, who has shared his extensive knowledge of the dharma and been helpful in many ways throughout the project. Special thanks to Tim and to Kimberly Johnson, each of whom read the draft of this book and offered excellent feedback and suggestions.

Thank you to Andrea Kleinhuber for insightful guidance on the book proposal, to Scott Edelstein for expert assistance with the contract process, to Rev. Michael Wenger at San Francisco Zen Center for prompt help with permissions, and to Emily Bower, my editor at Shambhala, for excellent suggestions on how to approach the editing process. Thank you to Tomoe Katagiri for her cheerful help with Japanese names and words and also some important details about Katagiri Roshi's life, and to Rev. Shohaku Okumura for quickly identifying the source of an elusive Dogen quotation.

Thank you to past transcribers and editors Yuko Conniff, Curt Dornberg, Steve Hagen, Willa Hathaway, Judy Melinat, Teijo Munnich, Clarence Sharpe, Flora Taylor, Kaaren Wiken, and others whose names were not recorded, for creating an archive of Katagiri Roshi's talks that I could draw on for this book. Thank you to Bill Borgen for his diligent work preserving and improving the audio recordings of Katagiri Roshi's teachings by converting them from tape to digital format, and to the benefactor whose generous donation made the conversion process possible. Thank you to Bob Williams for his expert knowledge of computers and steady support throughout my work on this book. And finally, thank you to the many people who have encouraged me by expressing their interest in Katagiri Roshi's teachings and their enthusiasm for what I was doing.

PART ONE THE COSMIC WORLD OF A MOMENT

Look at our modern life! Everything is moving quickly, and it's hard to keep up with the dizzy tempo. You try to find satisfaction, but no matter how great your effort, it seems you hardly make any progress. Finally you recognize that you cannot keep up with the bewildering, quick changes of time. That doesn't feel good. You feel uncomfortable, upset, or sad, and you want to escape. So you cover your eyes, turn your mind away from your dissatisfaction, and live your life based on having pleasure. That is modern life. I don't mean to criticize modern life, but something is missing.

The question of how to be free from the dissatisfaction and suffering of human life is a big topic in Buddhism. Many Buddhist texts explore suffering, and suffering was the subject of the historical Buddha's first teaching. In the Four Noble Truths, Buddha explained the nature of suffering, the cause of suffering, and the end of suffering, and then taught a way to be free from suffering called the Eightfold Noble Path.

Buddha said that to follow this path and experience liberation from suffering, first we have to see in the proper way and then we have to think in the proper way. Then he explained how we can liberate ourselves through the activities of speech, conduct, livelihood, effort, having a calm mind based on meditation, and concentrating the human life force. Buddha put seeing and thinking first, because to live in peace and harmony we have to see and think about life in the proper way.

When you see in the proper way, what do you see? You see the true nature of time. In Japanese we say *mujo*. *Mu* is "nothing" and *jo* is "permanence," so *mujo* means "no permanence" or "impermanence." Seeing impermanence is not to face a kind of nihilism that leads to despair; it is to become yourself, as you really are, with joyful open eyes. Thinking in the proper way is not to understand life through your intellect; it is to contemplate deeply how to live every day based on wisdom. When you see the true nature of time and understand how impermanence works in your life, you can use time to cultivate your life and to keep up with the tempo of life without feeling despair. That is the basis of a complete way of human life.

1   THE NAKED NATURE OF TIME

Eihei Dogen, the thirteenth-century Zen master who founded the Soto Zen school in Japan, always emphasized how important it is to see that human life is based on impermanence. In *Gakudo Yojin-shu* (Points to Watch in Buddhist Training), he mentions that the great patriarch Nagarjuna said, "The mind that sees into the flux of arising and decaying, and recognizes the transient nature of the world, is called the way-seeking mind." In *Shobogenzo,* "Shukke-kudoku" (Merits of the Monastic's Life), Dogen Zenji said that most people are not able to acquire the way-seeking mind of spiritual awareness without deeply understanding that a day consists of 6,400,099,180 moments.

This is a wonderful number. I don't know where Dogen found this number, but saying that there are 6,400,099,180 moments in a day is not talking about a mysterious idea; it is talking about something real. A moment is called *ksana* in Sanskrit. Sometimes we say that one finger snap has sixty moments, so one finger snap equals sixty *ksana*. A Buddhist dictionary may say that a moment equals one seventy-fifth of a second. According to the *Abhidharma* scriptures, a moment consists of sixty-five instants. The actual numbers are not so important, but we should have a sense of how quickly time goes.

According to Buddhist teaching, all beings in the universe appear and disappear in a moment. The term *impermanence* expresses the functioning of moment, or the appearance and disappearance of all beings as a moment. It means that all life is transient, constantly appearing and disappearing, constantly changing. You are transient, I am transient, and Buddha is transient. Everything is transient. Wherever you may go, transiency follows you. Transiency is the naked nature of time.

In day-to-day life you don't perceive the transient structure of time because your rational mind cannot recognize the flux of moments. The true tempo of time is too quick for your mind to keep up with, so you sense a gap between you and time. Then, because of that gap, you feel that your life is completely separate from the rest of the universe. When you sense that gap, you can hardly stand it; it is beyond bearing. You think, "Wow! How awful! What's the matter with me?" And you feel that you can never get along in your present circumstances.

All of us experience a gap between our minds and the reality of time—that's why we suffer. Then, instead of accepting the transient nature of life and facing impermanence with a way-seeking mind, we want to escape and find something that will satisfy us so that we can feel relief. But actually there is no gap between your mind and time, not even the space of a piece of paper. This is reality, fact. Even though your mind cannot keep up with the quick changes of time, you already exist in the domain of impermanence, together with everyone and everything in the cosmic universe. As a human being, you inherently have a great capability that enables you to realize this truth and to experience your life with deep joy.

To know this joy we practice looking at ourselves with a calm mind. That is Zen meditation called *zazen*. Through the practice of tranquillity in zazen, we can catch up with the quick tempo of time and, with a way-seeking mind, see deeply into what it is to be human. So if you want to know yourself and society as it really is and live comfortably in the transient reality of a moment, make your body and mind calm. Settle on yourself as if your body and mind were a huge building rising toward the sky from your round cushion. Open your mind again and again to see what impermanence means.

Buddhism teaches us to face the truth of impermanence and to accept the fact that life consists of moments that appear and disappear at superspeed. But it's not so easy to do this. We want to believe in the continuity of our lives so that we can say, "Yes, I exist!" So instead of looking directly at time itself, we try to escape the cruel fact that impermanence constantly cuts off our lives. Unconsciously, our minds decorate time with many ornaments in order to make our lives more secure and meaningful.

Using his own life as an example of this, in the *Tenzo-kyokun* (Instructions to the Cook), Dogen Zenji tells how, as a young monk traveling in China, he once encountered an old priest serving in the office of *tenzo,* or head cook. Dogen felt the *tenzo* was working too hard for a person of his age, so he asked him, "Reverend sir, why don't you do zazen or read the koans of ancient persons? What is the use of working so hard as a *tenzo* priest?" These questions come from Dogen's sensing the unbearable gap between his mind and time, and wanting relief. They show that the young Dogen does not know how to just be present and live comfortably in the transient stream of time. Instead, he is trying to make his monk's life meaningful.

If you become a monk, you ask: What is the purpose of monks? If you become a human being, you ask: What is the purpose of human beings? But no matter how long you try to follow a meaningful purpose in life, impermanence always cuts it off. When you realize this, you really wonder: Why do we have to live with effort? Why don't we just live as we like?

Dogen was looking for meaning when he went to China to find an answer to the question: If we are already buddhas, why is it that we have to do spiritual practice? That is really Dogen's question when he asks, "What is the use of working so hard as a *tenzo* priest?" He thinks the old man should forget about daily living and just do zazen or study the writings of the patriarchs. But Dogen is just creating ornaments.

Since human beings have been born in this world, we have decorated our lives with lots of ornaments in order to make time more meaningful. We develop remarkable civilizations of culture, politics, beauty, and pleasure. We create intellectual disciplines such as history, economics, science, philosophy, or psychology, and then we believe that they make life meaningful.

Maybe we believe that a spiritual life can help us find meaning. So we create ideas such as God, Buddha, universal energy, the last judgment and paradise after death, theology, mythology, or morality and ethics, and then we try to depend on them to make us feel that life is worth living. Century after century we have done this, trying to find real spiritual security through making time meaning-ful. But still there is no solution, because they are all just ornaments. We still ask: How can you make human life meaningful? What is spiritual security?

We believe that we *can* make time meaningful, because we usually suppose that time is running on a road from here to there, toward a certain destination, from 12:00 A.M. to 12:00 P.M. We believe there is a stream of time that flows continuously from the past through the present to the future, so we say that there is one beginning and one end to this world. Then we think that time goes from a beginning to an end with a particular purpose, and we expect that we can make progress and feel satis-fied as a result. But if you are seeking to know time in its naked nature, you cannot believe this because time is not a succession of constantly connected moments going to-ward a certain destination; in the transient stream of time, moments appear and disappear. Impermanence constantly cuts off your life, so every moment is separate.

I don't want to reject ornaments. There's nothing wrong with science, culture, and religion. Ornaments are important. Without ornaments you cannot exist. But if you take those concepts and ideas away, what's left? Just the transient stream of time! No matter how long you try to make your life meaningful, you cannot find a way to do it unless you face the original nature of time. So before you use ornaments, make those ornaments more meaningful by seeing deeply into human life based on time. Be present, from moment to moment, right in the middle of the real stream of time. That gives you spiritual security. That is why in Buddhism we don't try to escape from impermanence; we face time itself in our daily living.

Dogen went to China to study Zen Buddhism in order to enhance his life: to accomplish the main purpose of his life as a Zen monk and to make his life meaningful. Those are wonderful ornaments, but this is not the total, overall picture of human life. There is still something you cannot find that way because there are many things that cannot be made into ornaments. That is why the old monk said to Dogen, "Good foreigner, you seem to be ignorant of the true training and character of Buddhism." In other words, you don't know the real meaning of Buddhist practice or the real character of Buddhist scriptures. This gave Dogen a really big shock.

Later that year, the *tenzo* visited Dogen, and Dogen asked him, "What are words?" The *tenzo* said, "One, two, three, four, five." This answer indicates decorating life with ornaments in order to make it meaningful, instead of facing the real nature of time, where there are no concepts, no ideas, nothing to say. The *tenzo* is telling Dogen: Look at how you decorate daily living with lots of ornaments! Then Dogen asked, "What is practice?" The old monk said, "Nothing is closed in the universe." Saying that nothing is closed in the universe leads you to touch the core of your life, which is always present before you try to bring any concept or idea into it. It is saying: Do zazen! Dogen was really impressed by the old monk's answers and wrote, "I owe it entirely to him that I could, to some extent, grasp the true meaning of the character and discipline of Buddhism."

We usually look just at the surface of life, thinking we

can find meaning there. If you go to school, you might put lots of academic knowledge into your head and then take pride in yourself. You think that studying is all you have to do. It seems to be good, but it is just the small scale of life. It does not show you the overall picture of your life. If you are proud of yourself, maybe you won't care about daily living or other people's feelings or your relationship with your parents, nature, the kitchen, vegetables, and propane cooking gas. Of course you should go to school and study, but that is not all there is. Many things are completely outside the system of academic knowledge. There are many things you don't know, because life is really unfathomable.

Saying that life is unfathomable means your life is moving and changing from moment to moment. When you understand this at the conscious level, you feel melancholy. Sometimes you despair or feel hopeless. But if you feel that way, you are seeing just the surface of time, you are not seeing real time. What is real time? It is just a dynamic stream. The real nature of time is exactly the same as the real nature of impermanence. But there is no way to know impermanence empirically, because impermanence is not something you can understand with your cognition, feelings, emotions, or consciousness.

On the conscious level, the fact that you cannot understand impermanence conceptually is expressed as meaninglessness. Saying there is meaninglessness is not to say that life is meaningless, it is just to point out that real time is completely beyond any concept of meaningless or meaningful—there's nothing for the mind to hold on to. It is very difficult to be present right in the middle of real time because impermanence always shows us this meaninglessness. So how can we exist? How can we take care of daily living right in the middle of the dynamic stream of time? This is the point Dogen really wants to make. Dogen doesn't want impermanence to be just an idea. He wants us to put the real nature of time into practice in our daily life.

Buddhism is really hard, particularly Dogen's teaching. He gives you a very hard practice: Keep your mouth shut and look directly at impermanence! This living practice is called zazen. Zazen is not a way to escape from life by being mindful of something that is apart from the human world; it is the practice of being present in the real stream of time and looking directly at life itself. Zazen enables you to plunge below the surface and leads you to touch the core of your life. It's not so easy. But even so, you have to do it, because spiritual life originates from the direct observation of impermanence.

Observation shows you that you don't have to be upset and try to escape when you realize that time constantly cuts off your life, because there is another aspect of time. One aspect of time is to separate; the other is to connect. The aspect of time that separates you from others is the human world. The aspect of time that connects you to others is universal truth. You are connected with all beings in time, which permeates into every inch of the cosmic universe, and space, where everyone and everything exists together in peace and harmony. So you are you, but you don't exist alone; you are connected with others: to dogs, cats, trees, mountains, the sky, stars, Dogen, and Buddha.

Having the two aspects of separation and connection is called impermanence. It is called moment. This is the original nature of time. When you see this, you feel deep relief and live with a warmhearted feeling, because you understand yourself very deeply. You understand what a human being is. And you understand the one place, called the domain of impermanence, where you live alone and at the same time live together with all beings in peace and harmony. This is spiritual security.

3 TAKING CARE OF EXPECTATION

Spiritual security means you are fully alive and comfortable in your life as it is, without expecting anything. With a calm, way-seeking mind, you can face the naked nature of time, whatever happens, without escaping into your own ideas of progress or meaning, relief or satisfaction. This is the way to find real relief and satisfaction, but it's not so easy to do.

When I was a teenage boy during the Second World War, life in Japan was really unimaginable. Every man was called away to war, and high school students had to stop studying and go to work for companies making planes and boats. Sometimes teenagers had to go into the army, air force, or navy. Even I couldn't escape. So, when I was sixteen, I served in the air force, cleaning and taking care of planes.

One morning an air raid siren sounded suddenly at 2:00 A.M. All the soldiers immediately got up, got dressed, and went outside. I could hear the sound of the plane, so I rushed into an uncovered dugout. The entire area was bright. My friend next to me was as brightly lit as if it were daytime, and a big plane was flying above us. The next moment I heard the bomb coming down. If you hear a bomb coming down from the sky, you don't feel so well. At that moment I noticed that I was practicing the invocation of Buddha's name.

My parents were enthusiastic, serious followers of the Shin school of Buddhism, but in the air force I had never thought of invoking Buddha's name. But at that moment I did it, because I suffered fear and unconsciously wanted to escape. My subconscious mind made me think, "I want to live—I have to live." I made an invocation of Buddha's name, and my mind asked, "Please help me," but nothing happened. The invocation gave me no help. There was just the invocation, that's all. Fortunately it was a flare that dropped, not a bomb, so I survived. If it had been a bomb, probably I would already have said good-bye to this world.

When I invoked the Buddha, what did my mind expect? Consciously or unconsciously, I decorated the invocation of Buddha's name with the idea that Buddha would save me from my suffering. But in the domain of time in its naked nature, you cannot insert your own ideas or expectations into a moment, because by the time your mind works, that moment has already gone.

Like my invocation of Buddha's name, your mind decorates life with expectations. Maybe you think that if you practice zazen, you will find paradise. This is just your mind. When you do zazen, don't have any expectations. You don't know what will happen. Zen masters always tell you, "Don't expect enlightenment—just sit!" But have you experienced doing zazen in that way? You always look at your zazen and say to yourself, "What's the matter with my zazen? Hey, don't sleep!" But sleep is always waiting for you; a dizzy mind is always waiting for you.

It is the momentary structure of time that makes you talk to yourself that way. Impermanence creates a gap that makes your mind blink, so you want to escape. When you find it difficult to practice zazen, you're blinking. But don't escape! You can't escape the cruelty of impermanence, which is always cutting off your life, so watch yourself carefully when you realize that you're blinking. Try to face impermanence directly, with a way-seeking mind. I don't mean you shouldn't blink your eyes in zazen; that's okay. But, as much as possible, try to go ahead. Take one step without blinking your mind. Turn your mind away from the gap you sense from impermanence, and turn toward true impermanence. Stare at reality face-to-face, without blinking, and become yourself with open eyes. This is Buddha's practice.

When you practice zazen, no matter how you feel, just concentrate on breathing, without thinking, "My concentration is good" or "My concentration is poor." Whatever you feel, don't worry about it. Please just sit. Take care of your breathing with wholeheartedness. That's enough. Just to follow this practice is to live a significant life. Maybe you don't think so, but it's true. After you understand this point, if you are willing to practice zazen, that's good; I recommend that you practice. At that time you can settle on yourself with dignity, like a big mountain, and start to walk, step-by-step. But if you don't understand the fundamental nature of impermanence, and think there is something you can get from the practice of zazen, you will find despair.

Zazen doesn't give you something—it's the complete opposite! In zazen you will find many things about yourself that you never noticed before, things you did not want to see, so you hid them under many layers of decoration. When you start to practice zazen, something leads you to gradually take those layers off. What leads you to take off your layers day in and day out? Impermanence takes them off. Whether you like it or dislike it, the more you practice, the more layers of decoration you remove, without any reservation.

Sometimes you feel sad or pensive when you remove decorations and see zazen in its naked nature, because you realize the gap between your mind, which wants or expects something, and zazen itself. But that's all right. Just try to take one step forward without blinking, without falling to the ground. If you plunge into zazen and experience something unexpected, don't attach yourself to what you feel from that experience. All you have to do is take care of your posture and breathing with a kind, considerate, and thoughtful spirit. If you practice hard, and one by one remove the layers that cover you, finally there is nothing left to take off and nothing that separates you from other beings.

Without your layers of decoration you are a person who is completely transparent, like Casper the Ghost on television. Actually you are more invisible than Casper, because you have no form. You cannot say who you are, because there is nothing there: no concept of you, no concept of zazen. When there is no concept of you or zazen, there is just transiency, just time. So you are not you, you are time. That's all! You may be surprised or upset. But if you just watch yourself with a calm mind, you can see the truth that everything changes moment after moment. At that time, you can realize yourself as a human being who exists in the domain of impermanence, attain enlightenment, and save yourself from suffering.

4 MAKING YOUR LIFE
VIVIDLY ALIVE

Everything is constantly changing. No moment ever appears again in exactly the same way. None of the 6,400,099,180 moments of a day can be repeated, and nobody knows what will happen next. Many things happen suddenly—things that are completely beyond your control—and you have to take care of them, right now, with no choice.

How do you face a moment that is beyond your control? Imagine you are confronted with some event that happens suddenly. How are you going to face it? It is very difficult to face a sudden event. You may say, "Yes, I will face it with tranquillity and a calm mind." But I won't believe you, because a sudden event compels you to take an unexpected direction, beyond your intellectual ideas.

When I was in Eiheiji monastery, I had a very big shock: a big earthquake happened suddenly, just as the monks were about to leave the *zendo,* the meditation hall. The moment they began to step out, the earthquake started. Everybody was very surprised. The monks immediately ran away to some huge cedar trees in a vacant lot, where the big tree roots could protect them from the breaking ground. Even famous roshis ran to the trees.

Nobody seemed to notice that a candle was burning on the altar, but one roshi went back into the *zendo* and blew it out. This roshi was a monk whom others always looked down on because of his particular characteristics. But when the great Zen masters ran away, only he took care of the candle. He laughed and said, "Isn't it a terrible earthquake? Ha, ha, ha!"

I was in the middle of the hallway that goes through the kitchen to the *zendo*. At that part of the hallway there are more than twenty stone steps, and at the bottom of the steps there are two ponds and a bridge. If you cross the bridge, you find the big old gate, and through the gate you find the huge cedar trees. The moment the earthquake arrived, I thought, "Where are there some big trees?" Then I remembered those cedar trees. But I couldn't walk down the stairs because the earthquake was so strong. So I slid down on my bottom, passed under the gate, and reached the trees.

One of the roshis always walked slowly and would scold any monks who walked fast, but when the earthquake happened he also ran to the trees. One of my friends was the attendant to the director of Eiheiji. My friend rushed to him and said, "Earthquake!" The director was a very old priest. He began to leave, but he could not walk quickly. My friend felt he had to stay with him, whatever happened, because it was his responsibility. The director walked very slowly, without saying anything, until he came to the lecture hall on top of the hill. Then he said, "I don't want to walk anymore. I want to sit on the square cushion in front of the altar." That surprised my friend, and he said, "Excuse me, sir, I want to leave immediately." The archbishop of Eiheiji was taking a bath when his attendant rushed into the bathroom and said, "Earthquake, earthquake!" But the archbishop said, "Oh, earthquake? Just a minute, I am taking a bath."

From these stories, I hope you understand that when something happens that you didn't expect, you cannot always control yourself with a calm mind. When the earthquake happened, many monks and Zen masters were upset and ran away. The earthquake compelled them to run; it was beyond their intellectual control. If you want to develop the capability to live your life with a calm mind, study this situation. Try to understand the moment when the earthquake happened and why the monks could not depend on their intellectual control.

How can a moment be explained? It's pretty difficult to explain one of the 6,400,099,180 moments, but if you want to talk about it, what kind of vocabulary can you use? From the viewpoint of physics, maybe we say that a moment consists of elemental particles. Or from the viewpoint of mathematics, a moment consists of functions. But when the big earthquake happens, are you thinking about elemental particles? No, it's too late! Before you think about what a moment is, you have already run away.

Dogen Zenji looked at moments in a different way. He said that if you want to say something about what a moment is, say that moment is arising. In Japanese the word for *arising* is *ki*. *Ki* is a kind of energy, always coming up, like springwater bubbling up from under the ground. If you want to understand moment as a concept, maybe it is called *ki*. But actually there is no room to insert any concept into this arising. So, to explain moment, we can say *just arising* or *arising only*. Dogen said it is *kiya*. Dogen's use of *ya*, a strong affirmative, implies that he understood moment in a dynamic, nonconceptual sense. It is difficult to understand, but according to Dogen, arising appears as beings, the human world of existence.

If you try to understand the idea of existence in the usual sense, you may ask, "Who am I?" or "What is Buddha?" When you ask those questions, you are looking at yourself, or Buddha, as an object that you can analyze. For example, when I say, "I was born in Japan in 1928; my father was named Kashichi and my mother was Tane," I am seeing myself as an object. Buddhism doesn't see the self that way, because when I am present in the domain of impermanence, I can't say who I am. I realize from the bottom of my mind that I exist, but I can't say anything at all about myself because there is no concept there. At that time I am just arising. Before my mind starts to analyze who I am, a being arises, something named Katagiri appears, and I am here. I exist! So if you want to make a vivid statement about yourself, say you are *kiya*—arising only!

You can imagine what arising is, but your mind cannot catch that quick moment. So you still have questions: What makes arising appear as you, a particular being? What appears and what changes? Any explanation is evasive, because you don't understand that before you think about who you are, your whole body and mind exists in the stream of a moment. According to Dogen, everything that exists is time, so you are time. Dogen uses the phrase "the time has come" to say that time arises from conditions and appears as particular beings. Does that mean that everything appears by chance? No, in Buddhism "the time has come" is known as interdependent co-origination, or conditioned origination.

Conditioned origination is a complicated Buddhist idea that is difficult to understand. But simply speaking, moment after moment conditions produce "the time has come," and beings appear. What are conditions? Conditions consist of many physical and mental elements that become the five aggregates of worldly existence called *skandhas:* form, or matter; sensation, or feeling; perception; mental impulses; and consciousness, or mind.

Your individual life and personality are five *skandhas* that come together in a particular way, according to conditions functioning in a moment. When the five *skandhas* operate, the world of a moment appears, and when the five *skandhas* stop operating, the moment disappears. There is no permanent substance that is inherent in anything; the five *skandhas* appear or disappear, that's all. So your physical body, perceptions, and consciousness all appear and disappear with the transient moment and are always changing.

In the moment that the earthquake happened, many conditions existed around the monks and Zen masters, and they ran away. What made them run? When the earth moves, buildings make a terrible noise and trees fall down; a Zen master feels something, perceives it, and in the next moment his consciousness starts to work. He is afraid, and then he runs. The earthquake compels him to do it, beyond his control. So, did monks and Zen masters run, or was it just conditions that ran away? Do monks and Zen masters appear and disappear, or is it just conditions that appear and disappear? This is a very important point. The moment the earthquake happens, everything is equal—there is no permanent substance, there are just conditions arising and disappearing. So we say it is not Zen masters that appear and disappear, it is just conditioned elements that appear and disappear.

The monks and Zen masters are not substantial; they are transient. But according to our usual sense, we believe that something substantial does exist—Zen master. Then our usual sense starts to judge: He is a good Zen master because he was calm, or He is not so good because he ran away. If you praise or criticize the Zen master, you have already made him substantial, but actually it was just conditioned elements running toward the trees. It is not necessary to judge the Zen master as good or bad. Conditions came together around him, and the vivid moment compelled him to do something. This reality is called *kiya*. When *kiya* arises, a moment of existence appears. Existence arises in the reality that the time has come. And the reality that the time has come arises as the function of conditions.

How do you live in this complicated reality? How do you face the moment when the earthquake suddenly happens? How do you handle yourself in a moment that is beyond your control? When a moment appears, there is only one thing that controls you: the capability that comes from your spiritual practice, your ability to face impermanence and deal calmly with the conditions of every moment. So, before the earthquake happens, before your mind starts to work and you want to run away, accept every moment as an opportunity presented to you to practice facing reality as it really is. When a moment arises, you don't know the reason why it exists, but you have to accept it and face it, whatever happens.

Life is an emergency case! Where is the emergency? Is it a particular situation, one day of your life? No, every moment of every day is an emergency. You have to do your best to face every moment, because this moment will never come again. The moment that you are living right now is a very important opportunity to make your life vividly alive. If you want to live with spiritual security in the midst of constant change, you have to burn the flame of your life force in everything you do.

If you think that you have lots of time and many choices in your life, you don't believe me when I say that you have to pay attention to every moment. Maybe you will realize it if you become sick. But there is no guarantee that you will be able to face that situation with the calm, secure mind of equanimity, because you cannot get the capability overnight. That's why Dogen always emphasized that life is impermanent, using expressions such as "time passes quickly" and "birth and death is the vital matter." Dogen really wants you to take care of your life constantly, wherever you are, whatever you are doing. When you play sports, work at your job, write a poem, or whatever it is that you do, that is an opportunity to burn the flame of your life energy.

Taking care of right now is coping with an emergency case. So when a moment comes, whatever happens, just face your life as it really is, giving away any ideas of good or bad, and try your best to carry out what you have to do. You can do this; you can face your life with a calm mind and burn the flame of your life in whatever you do. This is Buddha's practice. That's why teachers always tell you to practice, devote yourself to doing something, and forget yourself. When you forget yourself and put your wholehearted effort into facing every moment, you can do something, and simultaneously you can rest in the continuous flow of life energy. Then you really enjoy your life.

You can enjoy your practice, but practice just for yourself is not good enough. If you practice just for yourself, you attach to the idea of getting something from practice. Then your expectations are endless, and you will never find peace. So your practice must be for everyone: you, other people, birds, trees, and all beings. Just plunge in and take care of what you have to do right now, before you think of yourself. When you make the effort to practice for all beings, something wonderful gives forth from every pore of your body. You don't know what it is, but it is a really great help. You can help other people in this way, and you can also help yourself. Then, whatever situation you are in, you experience a feeling of being completely present, very stably and securely, and you realize that a great power is supporting your life. That is spiritual security.

There is no better way to understand impermanence than the practice of zazen. When you practice zazen, just sit and take care of how you face the world of sitting on your cushion. Do it like a turtle: calmly walking, step-by-step, moment after moment, without expecting anything. Confine the monologue of your brain to the minimum.

Don't chase after thoughts or attach to feelings that you experience. You can't catch your mind, because it's one of the conditions of your existence—always changing. So go beyond the control of your ordinary mind and turn your mind toward the transient nature of the universe. Face the true mutability of worldly affairs and see yourself in your naked nature.

When you see your life through and through and stare at reality without blinking, that is called realization of the self. To live in peace and harmony, become yourself as you really are in the present moment as it really is. This is very beautiful.

5　RIGHT SEEING OF BUDDHA

The Buddhist way of seeing the world is quite different from the objective way that we usually see things. In the usual way of seeing, you look at a glass of water and say, "Oh yes, that is water." Then maybe your mind compels you to be curious, so you study what water is: a chemical composition of hydrogen and oxygen. In order to study it, you have already acknowledged that water exists as an object with substance. First you see that water exists, and then you study it objectively. The purpose of this scientific way of understanding is to have knowledge. Buddhism doesn't see water this way.

Of course, Buddhism doesn't ignore the existence of water, but the purpose of Buddhism is to save us from suffering. So it explains that nothing has its own permanent substance, because all phenomena in the world are constantly appearing, disappearing, and changing based on the conditions functioning in a moment. If you study water according to Buddhism, you may say, "Well, as a human being I think it is water for me to drink, but if I were a fish I would think that it is my house, my world. To me it is water, but to a fish it is not water." There are a hundred different ways to understand water, because a moment of existence is really complicated.

The understanding that water has no permanent identity is the difference between Buddhism and our usual sense of things. But even though we say that nothing has a permanent substance, when you pick something up, there is some substance there. So our minds are busy going in many directions, always picking up something to examine. The important point is not how to analyze water but how to face water vividly. When you examine something analytically, seeing it as an object, concept, or idea, you are not facing it vividly.

For example, you hear the sound of a bell. Then, unconsciously, you gather experiences from your past and create some thought. You think, "What kind of bell is that? It's not a Christian church bell; it sounds like a Buddhist temple bell. I wonder who is ringing it. It's a nice sound—I like it!" Instead of facing the bell vividly, you blink. When you blink, a thought appears. Then one blink creates another blink, and another blink. Moment after moment you create thoughts this way, and then you become attached to your thoughts. But attachment leads to suffering, because there is nothing permanent you can attach to. So Buddhism always tells us just to be present in this very moment and look. Just hear the sound of the bell. In the next moment, let it go. That's enough. If you blink and create a thought, in the next moment let it go.

If you try to examine your life analytically, asking yourself who you are, finally you will realize that there is something you cannot reach. You don't know what it is, but you feel the presence of something you want to connect with. This is sometimes called the absolute. Buddha and Dogen Zenji say true self. Christians say God. But even though you are aware that there is something you are seeking, it's pretty difficult to connect with it directly. That's why we practice zazen.

To contact true self, first of all make your body and mind calm and see the reality of how human affairs arise. When you investigate human affairs through and through, taking layers from yourself one by one, at last you realize that something is right in front of you, something that is open not only to you but to everyone. That is called moment. Philosophically speaking, maybe it is time, or transiency. Or maybe it is God, Buddha, or ultimate being. You can use many words to explain it, but it's hard to contact moment directly. How can you know this moment before you try to explain it using physics, mathematics, psychology, or philosophy? If you ask me how, I cannot tell you. There is no answer. If we have to say something, maybe we say it is unattainable. Does that mean it's impossible for human beings to know? No, there is some way.

There is a way to contact moment called *kanno-doko*, the way of rapport. Rapport is not something mysterious—it's very real. Buddhism tells us we should study and practice with a teacher because rapport is like a mother hen and her baby chick. The chick taps its shell from the inside at the same time that the hen taps the shell from the outside. *Bwaak!* The baby chick is born. If you want to seek for something that is unattainable, first you have to tap your shell from the inside. And then someone, or something, taps your shell from the outside. This is a very real way of practice, a very real way of touching truth and realizing your own buddha-nature.

How do you tap from inside your shell? All you have to do is settle yourself on yourself. Tap from the inside by facing each moment of time. This is zazen, just sitting. Concentrate on zazen. That's all you have to do. At the same time, your teacher taps the outside by facing each moment of time. Someday something happens. This *someday* is very important. Someday is the reality that *the time has come*. Someday is a great opportunity open to everyone. It doesn't exist apart from your life; it's right here, right now. But in order to realize that day, you have to arrange your circumstances, settle on yourself in zazen, and make the effort to tap your shell. At that time something helps you. If you don't tap your shell, nothing helps you. But if you do, you will realize that there is someone right in front of you who is about to help you. At that time you find what Buddha is and you find what the true self is.

In *The Lotus Sutra*, Shakyamuni Buddha says, "Come to me, come to me, open your eyes, look at yourself with open eyes." This is very important, but even though you read it again and again, you don't understand this short sentence. If you look at yourself with open eyes, Buddha appears. Buddhist teachers are always telling you, "Please take care of your life." So before your mind starts to analyze, accept everything that exists as the contents of your life. Open your eyes and see all beings vividly, as they really are, right now, right here. That is called right seeing, the first step of Shakyamuni Buddha's Eightfold Noble Path. After that, with a calm mind, profoundly think what you intend to do. Then, whatever it is that you do, do it wholeheartedly.

Zazen teaches you how to face yourself and how to face your daily life whatever may arise. When you practice zazen wholeheartedly and sit with dignity like a big mountain, even little children recognize something about you. Maybe they'll rush home and tell their mothers that you have become Buddha. This is true.

6   THE ROOT OF THE BUDDHA WAY

In *Fukanzazengi* (A Universal Recommendation for Zazen) Dogen Zenji gives particular instructions on how we should practice zazen: wear loose clothing, cross the legs and sit up straight on a cushion in a quiet place, breathe deeply through the nose, let go of thoughts, and so forth. But first he lets us be free from the idea that practice is something we do and then we become enlightened as a result. Dogen says, "The origin of the way is basically perfect and all-pervading, how could it be contingent on practice and realization?"

"The origin of the way" is expressed in Japanese as *domoto*, which also means "the root of the way." *Do* is "the way," or *tao*, the right path to be walked. In Buddhism, *tao*, or *do*, is regarded as *bodhi*, the Buddha Way, original enlightenment, the original nature of existence, buddha-nature, real reality, or truth. *Moto* means "the origin, or root." When we put the two words together, they mean that the way is the origin of existence; so Buddha's path is not something different from truth itself.

"Perfect and all-pervading" is expressed in Japanese as *entsu*. *En* literally means "round, or perfect," so *en* represents perfection, or the constancy of the nature of existence, which is omnipresent, pervading every inch of existence. It is with you wherever you may go. *Tsu* means "wondrous working with no obstruction." So, saying the root or origin of the way is perfect means that the origin of existence is constantly working, dynamically and freely.

Who produced this way that is perfect? According to Christianity God made it. In Buddhism there is no one to produce. If you say there is someone who creates or produces, you are seeing existence objectively, like the usual way of studying philosophy or psychology. But real life can't be completely understood that way. The main purpose of studying Buddhist philosophy and psychology is to be free from that objective observation.

According to Buddhist philosophy the way is produced by impermanence and interdependent co-origination. What produces impermanence and conditioned origination? That is time and occasion. Time and occasion are nothing but the activity of time, which is called time arising. What produces time and occasion? According to Buddhist philosophy it is emptiness, but Dogen says it is just *arising only*. That is a more positive way of understanding it. Emptiness, or arising only, means that real time is completely beyond time as an idea you can discuss. Time is identical with action, motion, or energy. There is nothing to hold on to, because everything in the universe exists as arising only. That is the meaning of saying the origin of the way is perfect and all-pervading.

When you practice zazen, the origin of the way is working freely and dynamically as the contents of your life, but you cannot understand it objectively because to understand real life is to be one with it. This is not only

Buddhist teaching; this is life. For example, if you want to be a cross-country skier, you can objectively understand what cross-country skiing is through research, but to understand skiing perfectly you have to go skiing. At that time the root of the way is dynamically working and you can become one with skiing.

Oneness with skiing is possible because everything lies in the one source of existence and is unified there. This is the place that is called Buddha or universal consciousness or whatever you say. This is the place where you are. The root of the way is present with you wherever you may go, constantly working freely in peace and harmony, so you can always use it. All you have to do is just tune in and accept it. That's why we practice zazen and try to refine consciousness of our minds. This way of practice is not based on trying to do something good and getting a reward. The final purpose of this practice is to leave no trace of individual experience. How do you do this? It depends on the attitude you take from moment to moment.

For example, when you want to satisfy your appetite, you have to take the proper attitude: make some food, set the table, sit down, take a spoon and eat, move your mouth. Very naturally, you practice. Then, when there is no food left in front of you, there is no trace of food and simultaneously there is no trace of hunger. There is just the total dynamic working between the food and your stomach, and your hunger is satisfied. Finally there is realization. That is just "thank you." It is feeling grateful for the food, for your stomach, for your mind, for your life, and for everything around the food and you.

In everyday life you cannot always regulate and harmonize your body and your mind. The only thing you can regulate and harmonize is your attitude. When you take the proper attitude toward your activity—zazen, skiing, or whatever it is—simultaneously, beyond your human effort, refined practice comes up and there is a total dynamic working between you and your object. That's why Dogen says, "How could it be contingent upon practice and realization?"

The practice and realization of enlightenment that Dogen mentions is very different from the practice and enlightenment you understand conceptually. It is completely beyond your intellectual speculation. So when you think that you aren't making good progress in zazen, or whatever practice you do, don't criticize yourself too much. All you have to do is follow the technique. Just continue to act! Day after day, moment after moment, just take care of practice, leaving no trace of technique and no trace of practitioner. This is a very fundamental attitude toward human life. If you do it, finally you will be great: a great skier, a great artist, a great musician, a great poet, a great philosopher, a great businessman, or a great religious person.

Dogen says the way-seeking mind must be aroused a hundred, thousand, million, or 6,400,099,180 times a day, day after day. But we don't know how; we don't know what kind of attitude we should take. That's why a teacher gives us instructions, techniques, and regulations. Follow these instructions and, very naturally, realization appears as final verification of your life. Realization is represented in Japanese as *sho,* which means "proof, or verification." *Sho* is not something to be verified by someone; it is the final verification of truth, of how your life is going on in real reality. It is feeling grateful for yourself, for your mind, and for everything around you. This is final verification. "Here I am!" That's all. That is completely wonderful. That is final proof of your life. You feel alive! There's nothing to say, but you feel good. It's more than feeling good, it's feeling that your life is worth living.

PART TWO

**PROFOUND
HUMAN DESIRE**

Human beings have a profound desire to know something fundamental, something basic. In the intellectual sense we don't know what it is exactly, but we intuitively know it in the spiritual sense. We want to be in the pure and clear state of existence that is always going on beyond our feelings of attachment, passion, grasping, or egoism. We want to be in that state of existence where there is nothing to attach to and all we can do is just be. Strictly speaking, the something we want to know is impermanence, the true nature of time.

But people love passions and emotions, so we usually deal with life using the aspect of body and mind that is based on ideas and feelings. We never give ourselves a chance to see the other aspect—the body and mind that is beyond ideas and feelings. When we don't understand that other aspect, suffering always comes up, and the things we expect will bring us relief and satisfaction just create more confusion and dissatisfaction. Finally, sooner or later, we want to know what is beyond ideas and feelings.

We want to know that pure and clear aspect of existence, but we always think of it as something that is separate from us, so we try to know it objectively. The problem is, impermanence isn't something we can see objectively because we are already part of it. We can be together with it spiritually, but it's too close to us to know it intellectually. Still, for as long as human beings have existed, we have wanted to know anyway. Everyone, regardless of whether we are wise or not, tries to know. Then, when we cannot know, we experience suffering.

We say "suffering" in English, but in Sanskrit the word is *duhkha*. The Dalai Lama translates *duhkha* as "unsatisfactoriness." That is really a better translation, but we usually say suffering. *Duhkha* has two meanings. In the common sense, *duhkha* is a kind of thirsty desire: a sensation of dissatisfaction that always drives you to approach or avoid something based on greed and hatred. In the deep sense, *duhkha* is emptiness: there is nothing to satisfy you. When you see suffering, it has already appeared on the surface of the conscious world. But at the bottom of suffering is the transient nature of reality itself. That's why *duhkha* is the first of Shakyamuni Buddha's Four Noble Truths.

In the conscious world of suffering your body may hurt or your mind may be uncomfortable, so you want to get something pleasant or escape from something unpleasant. You may find temporary relief from the transient aspect of life, but your needs and desires can never be satisfied for long because your life is based on impermanence. Your body and mind, your needs and desires, are always changing, so there is nothing to attach to, nothing solid for you to hang on to, and nothing that can give you permanent satisfaction.

At the bottom of suffering is time. Our ordinary minds

cannot catch the quick changes of time, so we feel a gap between ourselves and time. Then we believe that our individual existence is something that is completely separate from everything else in the universe. But this is a misunderstanding, which is called ignorance. Ignorance is a misunderstanding because in terms of reality there is no separation—everything is interconnected. Yet, because of ignorance, we experience ourselves as separate, and we feel dissatisfied.

As human beings, we always base our thoughts on this misunderstanding. We always feel that something is missing from our lives. We think that to live a peaceful life we must get something that is outside ourselves. Then we try to get it. But actions based on thirsty desire just become the cause of more suffering. That is why Buddha's teaching that suffering arises from desire based on ignorance is the second Noble Truth.

Buddha also taught that everyone has the capability to go beyond the ordinary body and mind and be fully present in impermanence with the whole body and mind. Then ignorance, desire, and suffering all disappear. That is the freedom we are seeking, the pure and clear state of existence where nothing is missing, the place where all we can do is just be. Then, from that place, truth comes up. From that place new life comes up. So let's accept our profound desire to be free from suffering and learn to touch the depth of human life that is beyond our ideas and feelings. That is how we can find real satisfaction.

Human beings are always searching for a way to feel satisfied and comfortable. So we produce countless experiences in daily life, good and bad, right and wrong. But no matter how long we seek interesting experiences, expecting they will give us happiness, our desires are still not satisfied. This is true even when we have good experiences, because we want to keep our good feelings around. We want to hang on to wholesome states of being because we know there are also unwholesome states of being, and we don't want to face them. So, whatever we do, there is always dissatisfaction.

We feel dissatisfied in daily life because there is time. In the stream of time our desires and experiences constantly appear and disappear from moment to moment, so there can be no permanent satisfaction. The functioning of time is something that is beyond human perceptual recognition, but even so it is something we have to understand through and through at any cost. Buddhism tells us that if we misunderstand time, life doesn't work: we don't feel happy; we don't feel comfortable. So we want to know what time is. But time is very strange. Time is not the long hand of the clock going around. Time is change.

In daily life you experience time because something is always changing. Even when you are alone in a room that is completely separated from the changing world outside, you feel time because your body changes. Time passes and your stomach feels hungry. If you could completely shut yourself off from physiological change, you would still feel time, because you have a constantly changing stream of consciousness.

Looking at it this way, maybe you would say that time is a constant stream of consciousness. But that understanding is a little shaky because your stream of consciousness is closely connected with memory. While you are asleep you don't see time. And sometimes, if you have a big shock, the stream of consciousness stops. Then one moment seems to be an hour because you completely lose the sense of time.

Would you experience time if you lived in paradise? People say that in paradise you live forever and all your desires are satisfied, so there's no need to seek anything. Can you see a stream of consciousness or feel time in such a situation? No, there is no sense of time there. Maybe, philosophically, there is something called absolute time there, but Buddhism wants us to know real time, not metaphysical time. Real time is closely related to the human life we are living now.

For example, in human life, if you take an examination at school, when the time is up you have to stop writing. Even though you think, "I want a little more time," there is no time left, so you have to stop. Or, if you become sick, even though you hope, "Please wait, because there is something important that I have to do before I am sick," it's too late—there is no time to wait. This is called impermanence. Whatever you think or hope, something is always changing.

What makes it possible for the world to change constantly? Buddhism explains three fundamental factors of impermanence: origination, extinction, and maintaining and destruction. Origination is to generate—something comes into existence. That is the appearance of life, the arising of moment as birth. Extinction is to cease—something goes out of existence. That is the disappearance of life, the cessation of moment as death. But can we say what the origination of origination or the extinction of extinction is? No, origination and extinction can't be understood separately; as independent concepts, birth and death don't make sense, they have no meaning. For change to occur there must be the third factor—maintaining and destruction.

Maintaining means that you accept your life in a basic way. There is no particular reason for accepting yourself. It's just that whoever you are, however you criticize yourself, you accept the existence of your life in an affirmative way. If you cannot accept your life, there is no hope and no effort to live. The fact that you make every possible effort to live in this world means that you have already accepted yourself. But maintaining doesn't satisfy you because simultaneously there is destruction. Destruction means that in daily living you experience death, because impermanence constantly cuts off your life.

Maintaining and destruction is also spoken of as continuation and discontinuation. According to continuation you see that yesterday is continuing to today, so you cannot say, "Yesterday is completely separate from today." Because there is continuation, you accept your life with hope and make an effort to live every day. On the other hand, you see that today is not yesterday or tomorrow, so you cannot say, "Yesterday is continuing to today." Because there is discontinuation, you look back over yesterday and see into the future; you reflect upon your past and desire to deepen yourself in the future. Then, very naturally, you move toward the future with your best effort.

There is a contradiction here: you accept your life, but you're never satisfied because death is also there. Why is human life so contradictory? Change. When we feel the process of change, we call it time. We sense time because there is change. Time as impermanence is the constant activity of origination, extinction, and maintaining and destruction. There is nothing to hold in your hand as a solid being, there is only the action of change.

How can we live peacefully in this world of constant change? It may be difficult for you to believe, but we should appreciate both maintenance and destruction. We are dissatisfied because of destruction, but that dissatisfaction is why we are willing to study and practice. And without destruction there could be no change. The destruction of one moment creates an opportunity for a new moment to arise. Because of maintenance and destruction we can have hope for the future and make every possible effort to deepen ourselves.

Change is the basis of human life, so don't attach yourself to birth or death, continuation or discontinuation. Just live right in the middle of the flow of change, where there is nothing to hold on to. How do you do this? Just be present and devote yourself to doing something. This is the simple practice of Zen.

When you start to practice zazen, you will see a panoramic picture of your life running through your head, from the past through the present to the future. Whatever it is, good or bad, right or wrong, it is right there. You may enjoy what you see or be disappointed when you see the unwholesome aspects of your life. But don't judge yourself by who you are or how you feel. Even if you feel something good, it is just experience; it cannot satisfy you completely. Sooner or later the panoramic picture will disappear because it cannot last. If you watch that panorama with some expectation, you just get exhausted.

In *Shobogenzo*, "Gabyo" (A Painting of a Rice Cake), Dogen Zenji commented on the saying, "A rice cake in the picture doesn't satisfy hunger." The rice cake means our experiences, and hunger is our human desire. The experiences we have in daily life are pictures created by our human minds; like pictures of food, they cannot satisfy our real hunger. But Dogen looks more deeply.

A painted rice cake is a rice cake that is produced by many conditions: sunlight, water, flour, and human effort. That rice cake can never satisfy your hunger because you cannot stop at one. You cannot stop eating, so the next day you want to eat another one.

Your daily life is also painted. A painted life is a picture of your life produced by your six senses (sight, sound, smell, taste, touch, and mind, or thought consciousness), your heredity, memories, customs, education, and many other things. You produce many experiences on the surface of your life, but then something changes and you are not satisfied. So you want to throw those experiences away and have something different. Human life is constantly going like this. You always evaluate and judge the surface of your life without looking at your life carefully and deeply, without thinking profoundly.

If you think something painted is not important because it cannot satisfy you, that's okay, but that is only part of the truth. It is a misunderstanding of human life, because when you think in that way you are only seeing human life objectively. If you only look at human life objectively, you are not participating in it. With that dualistic consciousness you create a big gap, and then you cannot catch up with life, which is constantly changing, so you are left behind. If you want to live in peace and harmony, there is something valuable that you cannot ignore. So let's see the rice cake more deeply. If you see the painted rice cake deeply, finally you can see the real rice cake.

The real rice cake is the rice cake as it really is, before you paint it with concepts and ideas. According to Buddhist teaching, real reality is the flow of continuous change, which never stops even for a moment. Can you satisfy hunger by this flow of continuous activity? Well, in the common sense, your first answer comes very naturally—no, no satisfaction. But if you deeply see the painted rice cake, you can see dynamic activity there, extending in every direction of the world. That means you see the depth of human existence. At that time there is no separate you and no desire to be satisfied, because nothing is separate from you. You just return to the basic nature of human life and see the total picture of reality.

Even though the experiences of daily life are just a panoramic picture that can never satisfy human desires, that panorama is right in the middle of the vastness of the universe. Painted lives and painted rice cakes are nothing but impermanence. If you touch the core of existence and understand what it means to say that the rice cake in the picture doesn't satisfy hunger, there is nothing to say. You are just present and you touch the real meaning of impermanence.

When you touch this basic nature of human life you feel relief. This is your final abode, your terminal station. If you take the train of human life, finally you arrive at the terminal station. It seems to be a dead end, but it is not the usual dead end. When you reach that terminal station it is the end, but it is also the beginning. At that dead end something happens. A new life comes up. From this basic place you can go anywhere—to the north, to the west, to the south, to the east—everywhere. Your life is open in all directions.

8   FUNDAMENTAL SUFFERING AS TRUTH

Human life is contradictory. We accept our lives and make an effort to live because there is continuation, but we are never satisfied because there is also discontinuation. A human being experiences contradiction in life, but an animal never does. If a lion wants to eat a horse, there is no question about whether it is right. The lion needs to eat the horse to support his life, so there is no contradiction there.

But when a human being wants to eat something, we do research: maybe it's right to eat meat; maybe it's not right. No matter how long we try to find the right reasons for something, there are still questions. This conflicting state of human life gives rise to reflection. Whatever answer we find, we reflect on it and ask, "Is that right?" or "Are you sure?" Human life is complicated, so we never find a completely satisfactory answer.

Everyone experiences reflection. It is natural. Reflection is a characteristic of human beings, and we suffer because of it. Saying that human beings suffer because of reflection means we are never satisfied. Yet for human beings there is no escape from reflection. Whether we like it or not, suffering is present in our life, because human beings have a consciousness that makes us reflect upon ourselves. Self-reflection makes you think who you are.

How does suffering come from reflection? From the point of view of time as impermanence, to reflect is to rebound. It means to arise from the source of existence and appear as a human being. Moment after moment we reflect when we rebound from the pure, clear basis of existence and appear as particular beings in the phenomenal world. Because of constant reflection we feel that we exist as separate beings, and then we want to know the source of our being. We want to know it, but the source cannot be grasped by our human consciousness, so we are dissatisfied and we suffer. This deep aspect of *duhkha* is not exactly the same as the suffering you can see in everyday life; it comes from an unconscious effort to investigate the root of consciousness itself.

Human beings reflect constantly, so there is always suffering. You cannot get rid of human consciousness. As long as you find an idea of yourself, you find the functioning of human consciousness. This is why we say that human life is characterized by suffering. But on the other hand, reflection deepens or enhances your life because it lets you go beyond the reality of your daily life. What causes reflection to constantly deepen your life? It is truth, the original nature of existence, which is called dharma. Dharma creates reflection, and reflection creates suffering and pain. But that suffering gives you many chances to investigate the root of your life and deepen your life in the dharma. That's why the Buddha said that suffering is truth.

Can you accept all cases of suffering as truth? You

cannot say, but still you have to do something with your suffering. In the realm of impermanence, you have to take care of suffering as truth. Because of suffering you can learn something. To learn is not to get something from an object that is separate from you. To learn is to be one with truth itself. When that happens, consciously or unconsciously you rebound: you touch the truth that is always present at the depth of your life, and then you bounce. Rebounding is just like water coming up from the ground, filling the bottle of your life.

It's a funny thing to say, but your life is like a big bottle. All you have to do is fill this empty bottle with wisdom. How? Constantly try to realize the depth of human life. Accept the fact that whatever you do, wherever you live, under all circumstances, you have a chance to realize the truth. With sincerity, try to realize the ultimate nature of your actions: bowing, studying, talking, or whatever it is that you do. When you bow in *gassho*, just do *gassho* through and through. If you really do this, you can touch the ultimate truth. Then through *gassho* you learn something. By the thoroughgoing practice of *gassho* you return to the truth, and simultaneously *gassho* rebounds in the form of your human life. Maybe you don't understand this now, but that *gassho* helps people and deepens and enhances your life.

If you realize the bottom of suffering, you will find egolessness and emptiness there. At that time impermanence turns into the truth. That is the experience called wisdom. Wisdom is a very deep, profound knowing. It is wonderful. But you cannot stay with the truth you touched because you must be right on the flow of impermanence, constantly one with the moment. If you stay, you die; your life becomes stagnant water.

So when you touch and deeply understand impermanence, don't stay with it. How do you not stay? Bounce! Touch it and bounce! To bounce is to rebound and then reflect egolessness and emptiness in your human body and mind. If you try to stay with it you become crazy, so you cannot stay. In zazen people sometimes feel they are going down into an unfathomable abyss, or the opposite, rising high in the air. Then they are scared because they seem to disappear. So if you touch something, don't stay with it. Touch the moment and bounce! Keep moving!

Touching the moment means touching truth. When you are touching the moment, you don't know it because there is no sense of *you* there. What you know is *after* the bounce. When you touch emptiness, you touch one side of a kind of partition. After bouncing, you touch the dualistic world on the other side. That's why Dogen Zenji said, "When one appears, the other one is in darkness." As long as you touch the moment, it's wisdom. When you return to the dualistic side and know that you touched it, it's not wisdom; it's faith. In the dualistic world, wisdom turns into faith.

Living in the dharma means we are constantly bouncing. This is our practice. In zazen you experience birth and death directly. Every single moment is birth and death, bounce, birth and death, bounce, constantly working. That is why bodhisattvas practice constantly. Continual practice means you are vivified, your life is really alive in the realm of dharma.

To be free from suffering, with your body just do

zazen; with your mind, think deeply. Look at the wonderful beauty of the world; see something more than the human world. You can see that beautiful world because you are already there. Practice this and finally you can realize the truth, because truth is not something separate from your life.

It is important to deeply understand human suffering because suffering and pain never go away. The more you practice spiritual life, the more you realize this. The more you try to live in peace and harmony, the more you see how egotistical and selfish you are. The deeper you go, the more you see the minute vibration of suffering coming up from the depths of your heart. It is true in every religion. If you pray to God with sincerity, you still suffer. Even though you attain enlightenment, suffering and pain are still there in your life. But that's all right. Just like everything that exists in the phenomenal world, your suffering is a being that arises from the original nature of existence, and every moment it returns to its source. So when you see suffering, all you have to do is accept it and offer your body and mind to ultimate existence. Then you and suffering return to emptiness and there is freedom from suffering.

9   TOUCHING THE PRESENT MOMENT

If you want to deepen your life and satisfy your profound human desire to know fundamental truth, what should you do? First, accept that your life is produced by the full commitment of the cosmic universe to movement. Buddhism explains the structure of the human world based on the functioning of interdependent co-origination, which means that everything is moving dynamically.

Interdependence is not the usual idea of relationship. It is a place where everything is empty and interconnected, beyond human speculation. Then, at that time, interdependent co-origination comes into existence as the contents of emptiness, and a new moment arises. Co-origination is working constantly, so from moment to moment your life is dynamically arising from the source of existence. That is *kiya:* just arising, the energy of time, impermanence appearing as your life. So accept it, demonstrate full commitment to life, and just be there.

Your life constantly gives you a chance, a great opportunity, to touch the truth. If you touch it, everything becomes alive in a refreshing way. This refreshing life is called flexibility, fluidity, or freedom. At that time you can really do something—something more than what you have thought. This is spiritual security. Spiritual security cannot be given to you—you have to find it yourself, and it can only be found within the source of existence that makes your life alive. That is called energy, or emptiness.

Most people misunderstand the Buddhist teaching of emptiness, thinking it means to destroy or ignore your existence. This is a big mistake! Emptiness is not negative; emptiness is letting go of fixed ideas in order to go beyond them. The Christian mystic Meister Eckhart called it the desert: in the desert of emptiness, everything dies and then comes back to life. This is really true. Otherwise you would not be successful in doing anything at all. When you dance, when you sing, when you walk, when you do zazen, whatever you do you must be empty first. Then your body and mind become flexible and you can really jump into painting, dancing, eating breakfast, washing your face, chanting, or doing zazen. At that time you become one with your activity, whatever it is, and do your best.

You and your activity already exist together in the realm of emptiness; you are not separate from each other. When you see yourself, your activity, and your body and mind in the realm of emptiness, occupying the whole universe, there is oneness. A beautiful flower is blooming. But there is no way to discuss that beautiful flower because it is beyond human speculation, concepts, or ideas. All you can do is pay careful attention to the reality of that flower as it really is.

To experience this refreshing emptiness, accept your life and then face it. Make your body and mind be fully present, and practice living with full devotion. Instead of trying to get something for yourself, totally offer your whole body and mind to whatever you are doing; surrender your life. To surrender means to let go of the idea that you have a completely separate existence and accept that your life is going on beyond your usual understanding. Then demonstrate full commitment from moment to moment and just be there. That's it! That's all you have to do. At that time you are right on the flow of impermanence.

When you are exactly right on the flow of impermanence, your body and mind are calm. The idea of a separate you, the desire for truth, and the experience of suffering all disappear in the moment. This is called egolessness. When you understand impermanence perfectly, you see that you and the universe are not separate. There is no space, no gap where you want to know something that is separate from you. There is no you and no particular thing to satisfy your desire, there is only constant change, the full commitment of the universe to dynamic activity. Full commitment leads you to touch what you are seeking.

What you are seeking is something that is beyond feeling and experience, beyond knowing or not knowing, beyond the conscious or unconscious level. When you take care of every object of your activity with full devotion, paying attention to the total contents of every moment, you can touch it. Then you realize how fragile human life is. There is nothing to hold on to because nothing is substantial. You see that everything is transient and nothing has its own fixed existence.

We can apply this to the zazen meditation we do. When we practice zazen, many things come up and distract us. So we have to take care of them continually, not with hatred, but by accepting them, just patting them on the head and passing by without being too interested in them. But if I pat my head and think "Good boy!" that is not the practice I am talking about. When I think "Good boy!" that idea is coming from an idea of "bad boy" I had in the past. If you see things this way, you are creating ideas, discriminating between the previous moment, the present moment, and the next moment, instead of being right here, right now.

When I say, "right now, right here" it means moment. We usually think of time as something that is separate from our life and moves from the past through the present to the future. But time cannot be seen as just time. Time must be seen as time and simultaneously as space. At the intersection of time and space, interdependent co-origination and emptiness work together and the phenomenal world appears. That intersection is called "right now, right here." In space, time has no before as a previous moment or after as a following moment; there is only the present moment, right now, right here, blooming and extending into the whole universe.

Right now, right here is a great opportunity. That is the moment you are you, as you really are, prior to the germination of thinking. For this you must be *in* time; you must be *at* the moment where you cannot think about a previous moment or a following moment. How can you do this? Just pat your ideas on the head and pass by. To pat their head means to just practice continually, just become empty and flexible. Then this emptiness makes your life alive in the universe and you are ready to act.

Buddhism is not a philosophical teaching—it's a teaching of human activity. We usually look at the activity of Zen practice with our consciousness, but true Zen practice must be completely empty. You can practice zazen prior to the germination of your intellectual sense and handle yourself before you are distracted by thought. Then zazen really works, and you work within zazen because your life is blooming in the universe. When you practice this way, your practice is simultaneously touching the source of existence and blooming your flower right now, right here. That is why practice is not apart from enlightenment—practice is enlightenment itself.

It's not a matter of metaphysical or philosophical discussion—you must be there. But you should also try to understand it theoretically as well as you can. Even though it is difficult, even though it makes your head ache, continue to study the teaching of impermanence. Even though time is beyond ordinary human recognition, try to understand it, because your life already exists there. You're completely free, but you must figure out a way to live and achieve continuity of practice day to day. If you practice, sooner or later you can feel something. Finally you can touch something deep.

We usually think we can escape from suffering and find freedom by satisfying our desire to get something or avoid something that is separate from us. But thinking that way is based on ignorance of our true nature, so actually it creates more suffering. Freedom from suffering is not found by looking at our lives from an egoistic point of view; it is found by seeing our lives from the point of view of moment. It is realizing that the moment we ordinarily see, which is the dualistic world of everyday life, is constantly manifested in the domain of eternity, which is the world of oneness, impermanence, and emptiness. Emptiness constantly becomes a new moment of life by the process of interdependent co-origination, so everyday life is nothing but eternity.

Buddhism describes interdependent co-origination as a chain of twelve linked and interconnected causes and conditions: ignorance, formative forces, consciousness, name and form, six senses, contact, perception, attachment (craving), grasping (clinging), being, life, and old age and death. According to this teaching, the three links of ignorance, attachment, and grasping are called delusions. Delusion functions within interdependent co-origination. So even though delusion causes suffering, through delusion there is always an opportunity to change your life.

In *Kyojukaimon* (Giving and Receiving the Teaching of the Precepts), Dogen Zenji said, "The threefold wheel is pure and clean, nothing to be desired. They go along together with the buddhas." Here the term *threefold* means body, mouth, and mind; sometimes we say body, speech, and thought. Another meaning is greed, anger, and ignorance. So the term *threefold* has two meanings: the body, mouth, and mind of human action, or the greed, anger, and ignorance of human delusion.

The word *wheel* is translated from the Sanskrit word *mandala*. A mandala is a kind of diagrammatic picture that represents the cosmic structure of life. In Chinese, *mandala* is *dan,* meaning "platform, or aggregates." In Japanese it is *rinengusoku,* where *rin* is "wheel"; *en* is "circle, or perfect"; *gu* is "with, in, or to already possess"; and *soku* is "being contented with." Strictly speaking, *rin* means "magnificent." *En* is usually translated as "perfect," but literally it means "circle." A circle is symbolic of the cosmic universe, which is endless and boundless, so I say inexhaustible. *Gu* means being endowed with everything. Everyone and everything is endowed with everything, so you are endowed with all— the universe. *Soku* means everything arises from this basis of existence.

When we put all the parts together, we can understand the threefold wheel like this: Each of body, mouth, and mind, or each of greed, anger, and ignorance, is endowed with everything and becomes the fundamental basis of existence with magnificent and inexhaustible time and space. Saying, "the threefold wheel is pure and clean, nothing to be desired" means that each of the three—your body, mouth, and mind, and your greed, anger, and ignorance—is already endowed with the functioning of the cosmic universe; everything is perfectly contented with itself because there is nothing to be contaminated by delusion. This pure and undefiled state of existence is going constantly, eternally, beyond human intellectual speculation. That is the basis of our existence. This is the point Buddhist scriptures mention constantly. And they emphasize that we should receive this truth, use it, and become one with it.

From an ordinary viewpoint we believe that body, mouth, and mind are contaminated, or deluded, not pure. That is a very common understanding of the threefold wheel in Buddhism. Greed, anger, and ignorance are, of course, deluded. If you see them from an ordinary point of view they become poisons: with the body, mouth, and mind we create a world based on greed, anger, and ignorance, and then we suffer. But in terms of clear-seeing buddhas and bodhisattvas, these are not poisons, they are wheels: the wheel of greed, the wheel of anger, and the wheel of ignorance.

How can you turn the poison of greed into the wheel of greed? Simply speaking, the Buddha taught that all are Buddha. We should accept this teaching, digest it, and make it alive in everyday life. That is called *jijuyu samadhi*. *Ji* means "the self," *ju* means "receive," and *yu* means "use." *Samadhi* is one-pointedness. So *jijuyu samadhi* means that you yourself receive the truth that all are Buddha and use it inexhaustibly by being present in the truth that all are perfect and pure. To turn the poison of greed into the wheel of greed, we should receive and use the truth that all are Buddha and constantly try to be present with it. This is your target to constantly aim at and move toward every day. This is the wheel of great greed, which makes your life totally alive.

Next, how can you turn the poison of anger into the wheel of anger? In *Shobogenzo,* "Sanjushichi-bon-bodai-bunpo" (Thirty-seven Auxiliary Methods for Realizing the Truth), Dogen Zenji says: "When the demon becomes Buddha, you should subdue him and let him become Buddha by dealing with the demon as Buddha. When the Buddha becomes Buddha, you should intend to become Buddha and let him become Buddha by dealing with the Buddha as Buddha. When the person becomes Buddha, you should harmonize him and let him become Buddha by dealing with the person as Buddha. You should know that there is a passage to freedom the moment when you deal with something as Buddha."

As long as demons exist in this world, they have their own reason to exist. That reason is completely beyond our human speculation, but demons exist in Buddha's world. So we have to find the realm of buddhas within the realm of demons. In other words, in the realm of pain and suffering, we have to find the realm of peace and harmony. This is religious practice. You cannot find any peace by escaping from human pain and suffering; you have to find peace and harmony right in the midst of human pain. That is the purpose of spiritual life.

The important point is: don't react quickly to pain and suffering with hatred or anger, because that is the cause of human troubles. Deal with demons immediately, but try to deal with them with a calm and peaceful mind, not with hatred or anger. If you become angry, as soon as possible make your mind calm. Be kind. Be compassionate. That is the practice of patience. If you do that, very naturally demons subdue themselves.

The moment when you deal with demons as Buddha, there is a passage to freedom. In the act of dealing with anger as Buddha, a passage opens to you. This passage is not something philosophical or metaphysical; it is the very concrete way you have to walk *now*, because that passage opens itself to you only when you deal with the demon as Buddha. At that time it is called the wheel of anger.

How can you turn the poison of ignorance into the wheel of ignorance? When you practice with no gap between you and what you are doing, simultaneously there is a passage to freedom and you realize emptiness—you realize there is nothing to cling to and no one to cling to anything. Your life becomes beautiful. In Japanese we say *todatsu. To* means "transparent, clear to the bottom of the water," and *datsu* means "emancipation, or freedom"—like a snake taking off its skin.

In *Shobogenzo*, "Kai-in zammai" (Ocean Seal Samadhi), Dogen Zenji says, "The great path of the Buddha Way is actualization and passage to freedom." Passage to freedom happens in the moment. There is a path to freedom in every moment. From moment to moment, actualization of emptiness and passage to freedom are working together in Buddha's world. It's beautiful, but you can't understand it with your head. All you can do is practice it every day.

Spiritual practice must be carried out quietly and calmly because a passage to freedom opens to you only when you deal with right now, right here. So under all circumstances, whatever feeling, emotion, or idea your dualistic human consciousness has produced, just accept it. Then, next, don't attach to it, just let it go, let it return to oneness. Then *you* can return to oneness. This is nothing but practice in action. This practice is naturally pure and clean. So right in the middle of sitting zazen, try to receive your body and mind and use them in peace and harmony. That is called the wheel of ignorance.

It is difficult to receive and accept oneness because human speculation doesn't catch it. But if you practice with full devotion, finally you will come to the final goal—silence. When you touch the core of existence and see the fundamental truth, there is nothing to say; you are just present in silence. This silence really makes your life alive. Then, even though you don't say anything, your silence has lots of words, demonstrating the truth in a physical and mental way, which can be seen by others. This is Buddha's teaching appearing through the form of a person who sees into the pure and clear depth of human existence.

11 A DEEP SENSE OF HUMAN VALUE

In Buddhist history the word *silence* corresponds to right view: seeing impermanence, the truth that everything is appearing, disappearing, and changing from moment to moment. Impermanence is not something you see objectively—it is something you taste directly. Then impermanence makes you silent, because impermanence is very quiet. That silence connects you with a deep sense of human value.

Silence is not just being silent. You are silent, but simultaneously there are many words, many explanations, and many representations there. Dynamic actions, both physical and mental, are there. In other words, silence is something deep and also very active. In Japanese the word for this silence is *mokurai*. *Moku* means "silence" and *rai* means "thunder." So silence is quiet, but there is an enormous voice like thunder there.

Shakyamuni Buddha kept silence when his student Malunkyaputta asked whether the Buddha would exist forever, whether the world is eternal, and whether the world is structured by spiritual or by material forces. Many people misunderstand this silence. To hear the Buddha's teaching of silence, we must examine the silence Shakyamuni Buddha kept in response to Malunkyaputta's metaphysical questions.

The first characteristic of Buddha's silence is emptiness. Everything is produced by interdependent co-origination, which means there is nothing to hold on to because everything is interconnected very closely, appearing and disappearing at superspeed. There is nothing but activity—dynamic functioning. This is called emptiness. When we chant the *Maha Prajnaparamita Hridaya Sutra* (The Heart of Perfect Wisdom Sutra), we say, "No eyes, no ears, no nose, no tongue, no body, no mind." In Buddhism we use the words *no* or *not* to show that nothing has its own separate existence, everything is interconnected and produced by interdependent co-origination.

The second characteristic of silence is oneness. Oneness is realizing the wholeness of existence instead of being content with knowing one small aspect. Silence as oneness is characterized by reflecting upon the self with an open heart that accepts and respects others. For example, to understand your own opinion you have to see your opinion in relation to other people's opinions. Then, when you see your opinion and others' opinions as one whole, it's pretty hard to fight each other. So finally you are quiet. When you deeply see who you are and taste human pain and suffering very deeply, you cannot say anything. You understand your own pain, others' pain, how each is connected to the other, how suffering is connected to happiness, and how all are related to your past life, present life, and future life. If you really understand this oneness, you can taste silence, you can see silence. When? Where? How? It depends on your practice. You have to practice being quiet. So instead of always discussing or arguing, be silent. I don't mean you should always shut up; I am talking about finding deep silence. Silence is a great space where you can accept everything.

The third characteristic of silence is devotion. Silence is full devotion—your self-centered life is thrown away to wholeness. A whole life is characterized by commitment in love, wisdom, and prayer. Prayer is not something directed from a particular subject to a particular object with the expectation of a particular result. Prayer is egolessness supported by deep love for all beings—a profound aspiration extended to all lives. It is the very basic, very deep energy of life. We must take best care of this energy and extend ourselves fully and deeply toward it.

The fourth characteristic of silence is magnanimity. Magnanimity is a kind of generosity or elasticity. Narrow views prevent this elasticity from working in our own and others' lives. For instance, if you say to me, "Katagiri, you're Japanese. I can't understand where you're coming from, so your Buddhism is not for me," that is not elasticity. You must be generous; you must be magnanimous. So try to be present right in the middle of magnanimity or generosity first. Then you can take a deep breath and realize the peaceful life.

Many teachings are found in Buddhism: impermanence, egolessness, interdependent co-origination, and so forth. But if you understand impermanence as something separate from egolessness or interdependent co-origination, it doesn't make sense. Impermanence can only be alive if it is backed by egolessness and interdependent co-origination. Buddha's teaching is very interesting because if you study egolessness, impermanence, or any other single teaching, whatever it is, the rest of the teachings are included. In other words, the rest of the teachings become the content of that one teaching. That's why we say that Buddhism is very vast. Vastness is a characteristic of Buddhism. It's vast and it's deep—there's nothing to pin down.

Buddha's silence is very important for us. So sit down in zazen. Put yourself right in the middle of the wholeness of the universe and be master of yourself there. Taste silence with your whole body and enter that wholeness with trees, rocks, and sky. At that time, each single form of existence appears, alive in the energy of profound aspiration.

The more you practice, the more wonderful flavors ooze from your study, your effort, your life. They are very tasty, but it's difficult to tell others how tasty they are because impermanence is not something you can pin down. You can talk about it, but talking doesn't exactly hit the core of your life. Talking is like leaning against a Japanese screen thinking it's a wall. When the screen falls down, you fall down. Like a screen, words and forms are impermanent, but people always lean against them.

For instance, if you come in from the cold and put your body and mind in a hot bath, you immediately say, "Aaahhh!" Then you lean on the pleasure of "Aaahhh" and completely forget the immediate experience that triggered it. What's there before you say "Aaahhh"? What's going on there? Your body doesn't exist as something that is separate from the bathtub, winter, and all things. All beings are the contents of your life. Experiencing that is oneness. Then you say "Aaahhh!" The moment you say "Aaahhh," your dualistic mind has already appeared.

If you depend on the dualistic "Aaahhh" instead of the experience of oneness itself, your life is always restless. You look at silence, truth, Buddha, or God, but you see everything in a dualistic sense. You may feel happy practicing Buddha's teaching, but something unsatisfactory is still there. There is a disconsolate flavor, something pensive that you cannot wipe out. That is the deep suffering called *duhkha*. Whenever you seek the truth or investigate who you are, you always see this suffering because you have a human consciousness. Most people try to erase or wipe out sadness and pensiveness, but you never can. You cannot wipe it out. The more you try, the more pensiveness and sadness you see.

Painters and poets try to express silence using materials or words, but they cannot do it completely. Whatever they do, they always experience a lack of complete satisfaction, because silence is not something that can be completely expressed by a painting or a poem. So a painter or a poet is never satisfied. Again and again they try to touch the truth and then express the deep meaning of their subject's nature. They do this in order to show the meaning of human life in their work. This is their practice. But there is always a disconsolate flavor there. They cannot do anything about it—they can only acknowledge it.

A deep, disconsolate flavor is always present in human life. At the bottom of your life there is something like moaning; you just make a noise, "*Oooooooh!*" You cannot stop that suffering. But you can go beyond it and see human life in a different way. If you see the aspect of body and mind that is beyond your dualistic feelings, emotions, and ideas, you can realize freedom from suffering.

To do this, all you have to do is settle down on the ground of human life, depend on that sadness to be there, and accept it. Deal with sadness, or happiness, with patience, zealousness, and understanding. In other words, try to deepen your experience of life again and again. If you talk, picking out one thing, your talk is already noise. Even if you talk about oneness, that talk is noisy. So just practice sitting right now, right here in silence. That is Buddha's full teaching.

As a human being, you have the profound desire to be free from suffering and know oneness. But real oneness is not something you can understand objectively; you must become one with it. Through your life you can touch the depth of existence. Zen teaching emphasizes right now, right here, because you always have the opportunity to touch silence right where you are this very moment.

When you are just sitting in zazen there is nothing to say, there is just silence. That silence is your life and also others' lives, which have become the contents of your life. All are interconnected and interpenetrated. When you taste this, very naturally your life becomes fully alive. Then you really understand your life, you express it, and you help others. The deep, disconsolate flavor will turn 180 degrees, and you will find joy.

PART THREE

TIMELESS FREEDOM

We cannot ignore time. Time is something very conspicuous in our lives. We live in the realm of time, so we have to think about it from many different angles: intellectual, emotional, psychological, and empirical. The problem of time is important philosophically, but it is also important to consider time religiously. Dogen Zenji in particular constantly emphasized how important it is to think about time in a practical way and to understand how time influences human life. Dogen's view of time was quite different from a philosopher's point of view, because his understanding of time came from a very profound experience of Buddha's teaching.

Usually we think of time in the common sense, as a stream running from the past through the present to the future. We think that way because we base our idea of time on the law of cause and effect. If someone hits you, you feel pain, so your human consciousness creates an idea of time that connects the past, present, and future. Then you believe that time is passing quickly and is characterized by the continuous existence of separate beings.

But that is a narrow understanding of time, which creates lots of problems and lots of suffering, because when you think about time that way, you become egoistic. You believe that another person's time is separate from yours and that you only have to take care of your own time. Then you feel isolated and cold. You don't feel a warm relationship with other people or beings and you can easily hurt them.

When we see human life only from that narrow view of time, we are blind to the total picture of time. This is a big problem. It is like always climbing a mountain and never seeing the mountain from a distance. Sometimes, to understand the life of the mountain, you have to see the beauty of the mountain as a whole, connected with the clouds and the sky. We cannot ignore or escape from the stream of time. We must be there. But we cannot be blind.

In *Shobogenzo*, "Uji" (Being-Time), Dogen Zenji says: Open your eyes and let's see time from a different angle! When you see your life from the broad view of time, you see that your life is not something separate from time— your life is time.

It is very important to see your life not only from the narrow view of your egoistic telescope but also from the broad view of the universal telescope called egolessness. This is why we have to practice. Right in the middle of the stream of time, we have to open our eyes there and see the total picture of time. Through spiritual practice we can go beyond our egoistic point of view. We can touch the core of time, see the whole world in a moment, and understand time in deep relationship with all beings. Then we cannot be isolated and cold people. We become beautiful and warm people, appreciating and helping all beings. That is why Dogen always emphasized seeing time in a deeper way.

Dogen Zenji's view of time is very difficult to understand. No one else has expressed the meaning of time exactly the way Dogen did. So when you read "Being-Time," probably you don't understand it. But even though it's difficult, try to get a taste of it. Try to understand, because through the words Dogen is expressing his deep experience of time. He is compassionately showing us how to make time alive in our lives. Dogen really wants us to understand how time influences human life so that we know how to live in the best possible way.

When you understand how the various aspects of human life unfold in a moment, you can live freely in the realm of time. You can face the moment and know what to do. Then, through conscious action, you can create your life, and your life really works.

12   TIME, SPACE, AND BEING

In the common sense, time seems to be something separate from beings, but Dogen Zenji says this is just our
idea of time, a provisional picture we create, not the total
picture of time. Dogen understands time in terms of all
sentient beings. He says that time must be considered in
relation with all sentient beings because time can be cor-
rectly understood only in deep interrelationship with all
sentient beings. The phrase "all sentient beings" means
not only human beings but also everything that exists,
animate or inanimate, visible or invisible, in the vast expanse of the universe.

According to Buddhist teaching, everything exists together simultaneously in a moment. This is not the usual
way of understanding human life, but you are always experiencing this in your life because you can think of
many things simultaneously. Simultaneously, in a moment, you can think of anything because everything is
there. You can think of Eiheiji monastery in Japan, you
can think of heaven, you can think of hell.

A dream is a good example. When you dream, many
beings come together into the moment. You might see
someone who existed in the past, ten or twenty years
ago, and also someone you could meet in the future.

When I was a child, I dreamed that I was on a train and needed to use the toilet. It was difficult to find the toilet because the train was jammed with people. I tried to get through them, but it was too difficult. So I tried to get off the train, but it was impossible. Somehow I did it anyway. I got off the train, found a forest, and relieved myself there. I felt a wonderful relief and simultaneously I woke up. I was in my bed! I couldn't understand how all these things could be connected, but it was a fact. The train, the people on the train, finding a forest—many things existed simultaneously in a moment.

Time seems to be separate from beings, but actually there is no separation. From moment to moment, all sentient beings exist together as a completely independent moment of time. When the moment begins, all sentient beings temporarily appear as particular beings in the stream of time and seem to have their own separate existences. When the moment ceases, all sentient beings disappear, but they do not go away; they are interconnected smoothly and quietly in timelessness. Dogen's word *being* represents all sentient beings existing in the formless realm of timelessness, and *time* characterizes the existence of completely independent moments. Being and time work together, so Dogen doesn't separate them; he uses the one term *being-time*.

But the total picture of time cannot be understood only in terms of being and time; it must also be understood in terms of space. Space is the vast expanse of the universe where everything exists. Dogen's understanding of space is not our usual understanding. According to our usual understanding, when something exists it takes a place that is a portion of space. We understand existence as something opposed to space. But that is dualistic thinking. If everything exists together simultaneously in a moment, then everything can't occupy a portion of space, everything must occupy the whole of space.

When we say "being," it means all sentient beings exist in space and occupy the whole of space. Being occupying the whole of space is called timelessness. Timelessness is a sort of energy that links the whole universe without creating any gap. In the realm of space as being, all sentient beings exist, but they are not separate; they are dynamically interconnected and interpenetrated in peace and harmony.

Yet we can't understand life just according to being, becoming attached to a fixed idea of space as being and thinking that time is not also there. If we say so, our life can't move at all. Nothing has a fixed existence, so being must also be no-being. No-being means being disappears into the arising moment and becomes one with time. When being is time, being manifests as the particular forms of the phenomenal world, and time occupies the whole of space as the present moment.

But in order for life to change, there must be another moment. So time must be no-time. No-time means the present moment returns to timelessness and becomes one with being. When time is being, time is nothingness. Nothingness has no form, it is just functioning energy. All sentient beings are dynamically interconnected and interpenetrated by the energy of timelessness, and being occupies the whole of space. When all sentient beings are interconnected in timelessness, the next moment can begin. Then being manifests itself anew as the phenomenal aspect of a fresh moment. So the source of time is being, and the source of being is time, but both depend on space. This is the total picture of time that Dogen really wants us to understand.

We say that human beings are just particular beings located at the intersection of time and space. You cannot separate time from space or space from time, but you cannot think of them as a combination. You have to think of time and space separately, but you cannot understand time separately from space. The intersection of time and space is called "right now, right here." At the intersection of time and space, time and space come together and work together mutually. We don't know how, we don't know exactly what happens, but it's a fact. This is reality. This is the place called truth, or nonduality, the place where you can see the overall picture of existence.

If you see the intersection of time and space, you experience complete freedom of being. This state of existence is completely beyond any idea of time, space, or being. In that liberated state you can see fundamental truth and the phenomenal world simultaneously. That is called Buddha's world. That is the place where all sentient beings exist, so you can stand up there and see all beings, myriad beings. Then you know very clearly, through your own emotional and intellectual understanding, how all beings exist.

13 THE PIVOT OF NOTHINGNESS

In "Being-Time," Dogen Zenji constantly encourages us to see time from a different angle by being present at the source of time. The source of time is the place where you can see your human life from a broad view. We usually think of time as streaming from the past through the present to the future, but at its source time is not like that. There is no stream of time from the past through the present to the future.

The past has already gone, so it does not exist. The future has not yet come, so it also does not exist. So the past and future are nothing, no-time. Then is the present all that exists? No, even though there is a present, strictly speaking the present is nothing, because in a moment it is gone. So the present is also nothing, zero, no-time, no-present, no form of the present. But that nothingness is very important.

Nothingness means total functioning, just functioning energy. When the present is no-time, it is interconnected with all sentient beings in the peace and harmony of timelessness. But when nothingness functions, there is a pivot, and it becomes the present. That pivot is called the pivot of nothingness. At that precise point—the intersection of time and space, which is called right now, right here—all sentient beings come together into the moment and a vast world comes up: past, present, future, earth, trees, planets, moons, and suns. In one moment, every possible aspect of human life, everything we can be, spreads out, unfolds, and a huge world comes up. That is called interdependent co-origination. Life is always at the pivot of nothingness; it is always right now, right here. Right now, right here is the eternal moment of the real present.

The real present is not exactly what you believe the present to be. In everyday life we constantly create some idea of what the human world is because we are always thinking of how things were in the past or how things will be in the future. When you are thinking about the past and future, the contents of the present are just imaginary pictures of the past and future, pictures fabricated by your consciousness at the pivot of nothingness, so it is not the real present. The real present is the full aliveness that exists at the pivot of nothingness before your conceptual thinking creates an imaginary world through human consciousness. So, to understand the present as a pivot of nothingness, your concept of the present must be negated. It must become no-present; then you can see the real present.

For instance, I have a *kyosaku* (wake up) stick. When I hold that stick maybe I think, "This stick was made more than twenty years ago, so I'd better make a new one." Twenty years ago implies the past; making a new one implies the future. So now, in the present, I am looking at the stick as the past and the future instead of allowing the present to manifest itself as it really is. That makes my life uneasy or unstable. But on the other hand, if I can just be here with this stick before my consciousness starts to work and I fabricate some idea of the past, present, or future, then the stick and I are fully alive together in the real present.

Even though you believe that the past, present, and future are separate because you can think of them as separate ideas, the real present is related with the past and future simultaneously, not separately. How is it possible for the past and future to exist simultaneously in the present? How can the present exist with the past and the future? It is possible because when time is no-time, time doesn't move according to common sense, time moves anywhere: to the top, to the bottom, to the right, to the left, from today to yesterday, from yesterday to tomorrow. There is nothing to pin down, no concept of time based on cause and effect, just total functioning energy.

You don't believe this, so you attach to your usual concept of time. But what is your concept of time? When a moment begins and all sentient beings appear as the particular aspects of the human world, your concept or idea of time is also a being that appears. When the moment ends and all sentient beings disappear, your idea of time also disappears. This means that anytime, anywhere, you can be free from your idea of time.

When you are right on the pivot of nothingness, free from the pictures created by your consciousness, you see time from a universal perspective. There is no gap where you feel separate from time, because your life is the whole dynamic world of time, and all sentient beings are the contents of your life. This is called egolessness. From that point of view, you see that real time is completely nothing, it is just a dynamic working process, functioning, going constantly. And you understand that your individual, human life is not something completely separate from others' lives; it is manifested in the vast universe together with all sentient beings.

14   REAL TIME AND DAILY LIFE

Life at the pivot of nothingness is nothing but motion and process. Through spiritual practice you can really understand this and enjoy your life. But no matter how long you think about it logically, you won't understand, because thinking always creates a gap. Then your daily life is not grounded in the real present; it is up in the air. You are mixed up and your life is really suffering.

In daily life we manifest the past as memory, heredity, or tradition, and the future as plan, prediction, hope, or perhaps ambition, and then we feel uneasy. We cannot ignore the past and the future, but we also cannot ignore the fact that Buddhism tells us those manifestations are nothing but pictures drawn by our consciousness. So what should we do? How can we see real time?

We cannot see real time unless it is manifested in daily life because real time is nothing but function and process. So if we want to know real time, we have to learn what it is through everyday life. Your daily life is exactly the same as the source of human life. Being in the stream of time is exactly the same as being at the source of time. To understand this, we have to stand up in the dynamic working process at the pivot of nothingness and do something with wholeheartedness.

In *Shobogenzo,* "Kai-in zammai" (Ocean Seal Sama-dhi), Dogen Zenji says that when you swim on the sur-face of the ocean, your foot touches the bottom of the ocean. In common sense this is impossible, but it is really true. The surface of the ocean is the human world in the stream of time, the huge world we create through our memory, imagination, ambition, hope, and plans. That surface of everyday life is rooted in the absolute reality at the bottom of human life. Your foot already touches the bottom of the ocean, you are already walking there, but you don't believe this.

We don't believe that our life is walking on the bottom of the ocean because we are always living on the surface, hanging on to the past, present, and future. We think the bottom of the ocean is something other than daily life. But we cannot ignore the fact that our life in the stream of time is constantly changing. It is constantly changing because it is manifested from moment to moment at the pivot of nothingness. So if you want your life to really work, then whatever you do—dance, art, painting, pho-tography, or sitting zazen—your life must be swimming on the surface, and simultaneously it must be rooted, walking on the bottom of the ocean. That is living wholeheartedly.

When we live wholeheartedly, we can create many as-pects of human life. This is a little difficult to understand, but actually you often experience this in your daily life. For example, if you graduate from the university and re-ceive your PhD degree, you may think you have reached your final goal, and now you can stop learning. But I don't think you can stop learning. The PhD is, of course, something you have achieved, but you cannot stay with it. In the next moment something changes and you must learn more. You live in a huge world that is constantly changing, and you share your life with all sentient beings in many ways. Something always compels you to move forward, and you really *want* to learn more. That means you have to move! Then, when you take step after step wholeheartedly, your life really works, and you constantly deepen your life.

When I try to explain it using words, it seems to be difficult. But I don't think it is difficult. You can do it! This is our practice. When you do zazen, whatever you are thinking, just practice zazen. Very gradually you can understand my words. Do zazen until there is no gap between zazen and you. Finally, "Aha! This is the pivot of nothingness!" Even though you don't understand now, just accept the words and keep them in your mind. Then if you see the total dynamic functioning at the pivot of nothingness, the place where all aspects of human life unfold, there is no confusion, no suffering, and you can live freely in the stream of time.

15 COMMENTARY ON AN EXCERPT FROM DOGEN'S "BEING-TIME"

Dogen Zenji understands time in terms of four key points: time, being, illumination, and the self. When we understand time in the usual way, it's pretty hard to have deep communication with friends, parents, trees, birds, nature, and all sentient beings because we feel separate and independent from others. We become egoistic and selfish, always seeking individual success. Then we suffer, because from moment to moment this kind of time is always chopping everything into pieces.

If you want to understand the stream of time in which you live, you cannot ignore the other aspect of human life: the realm of space, because the origin or depth of time is space, or being. This means you do not live independently; your life is connected with all sentient beings. If you ignore this aspect of human life, you cannot live in peace and harmony. So you have to understand that time is not time separate from space, or being; time is exactly space. That is why Dogen always emphasizes time with space.

You can separate time from space if you analyze human life intellectually. But in terms of the reality of life, which is fully alive from moment to moment, time and space are exactly one. The unity of time and space, the unity of time and being, is operating dynamically, so you cannot separate them at all.

You can really see this! When you open your eyes and see the world in the universal perspective, you realize this point. That is called illumination. Illumination means the unity of time and space penetrates your skin, muscle, and bone and illuminates your life, just like a light. You see the dynamic function of time and space, and then the unity of time and space is not a philosophical idea; it becomes illumination. Seeing the total functioning of time and space simultaneously gives you a deep feeling of appreciation toward human life. That is really wonderful inspiration.

But illumination is not something just for your own inspiration. It must be made alive within the self. When illumination is working in the self, it doesn't appear as something separate from the self. Illumination is not an idea that the self can look at, see, hear, or feel. No! Illumination must *be* self; self must be illumination. So when you see the unity of time and space, next you have to receive that inspiration and constantly make it alive as your life.

Making inspiration alive in your life is just practice carried on day by day. That is the final goal that Dogen Zenji always emphasizes. Dogen says: see something with wholeheartedness; hear something with wholeheartedness. Without this actual practice, you cannot make illumination alive in your life. Please remember this point. Dogen Zenji emphasizes this point as the significance of time. He uses a particular term: being-time, but it's not a philosophical concept.

Being-time means the complete oneness of time and space, dynamically functioning from moment to moment as illumination that is alive in the individual self. So the four—time, being, illumination, and the self—completely come together and work dynamically in your life. This is the unity of time and being. So remember this point. Then when you read this passage from *Shobogenzo*, "Uji" (Being-Time), maybe you can get some hint of Dogen's meaning.

BUSYNESS AND TRANQUILITY

Dogen Zenji begins "Being-Time" with the statement: "An ancient Buddha said: 'Being-time stands on top of the highest peak; being-time goes to the bottom of the deepest ocean; being-time is three heads and eight arms; being-time is the height of eight or sixteen feet; being-time is a staff or a whisk; being-time is a pillar or a lantern; being-time is the sons of Chan and Li; being-time is the earth and sky.'"

Then Dogen comments: "Being-time means that time itself is being. Every being is time. The sixteen-foot golden figure is time; because it is time, it is the grandeur and radiant illumination of time. You must learn that it is twelve hours of nowness. Three heads and eight arms is time; since it is time it cannot but be identical with twelve hours of the present."

Saying "time itself is being" means take off your colored glasses and let's see time from a different angle! This time is no-time, nothingness, interconnected and interdependent with all sentient beings in space. That is the characteristic of space called being. Being is the place where our usual idea of time can exist as no-time and become a pivot of nothingness. We may think that if time exists in space, it occupies a portion of space. Then we think of time as something opposed to space. But in order for time to become a pivot of nothingness, time must become the whole of space as no-time.

For instance, when I do zazen, if zazen is just a portion of me, then zazen is opposed to me and I am always looking at zazen. If I am always looking at zazen, I cannot become egoless because that "I" always thinks about zazen, then criticizes, judges, and evaluates the zazen I am doing. Zazen and Katagiri are dualistic, and this is always egoistic. At that time, Katagiri is a portion of zazen and zazen is a portion of Katagiri.

In order to become the egoless no-Katagiri, I have to occupy the whole of zazen; I have to become completely one with zazen. Then there is no-Katagiri and no-zazen. No-Katagiri means exactly zazen. No-zazen means exactly Katagiri. When the idea of Katagiri and the idea of zazen are completely empty, just the functioning of zazen appears. The same applies to Dogen's statement "Being-time means that time itself is being." That time doesn't occupy a portion of space; that time is the whole of space. Then time becomes a pivot of nothingness.

When Dogen says, "Every being is time" it doesn't mean everything is manifested in the stream of time, as we usually understand it. It means everything is reflected in the mirror at the pivot of nothingness. That is the vastness of the universe. It is very clear, very pure, just like a mirror. When you see your life reflected in that mirror, this is egolessness.

We have to practice egolessness constantly. We don't believe this because we are used to living in the stream of time, which is always facilitating the growth of ego. You may practice zazen for ten years, twenty years, and attain enlightenment. Does that guarantee that you are free from ego? Watch out! You don't know how strong the ego sense is. At any cost, we have to deepen our understanding of time and turn the egoistic sense of time into no-time. If we continue to practice, very naturally we reach the bottom of time. This is the pivot of nothingness, where everything is reflected without any sense of ego.

To see ourselves reflected in the mirror at the pivot of nothingness we have to throw away our ideas, our wishes, whatever it is: I want to attain enlightenment, or I don't want to be deluded. We have to forget it! When you do zazen, just do zazen until you become completely one with the full function of zazen and there is no egoistic sense that "I" do zazen. Then zazen is not separate from time, zazen is one with time. Zazen reflects in the beautiful mirror of not seeing from your own telescope, and just zazen appears. Then we can say zazen is you; you are zazen. We do this zazen, but it is not our zazen; neither is it *not* our zazen. Whatever we say, there are no words that hit the mark of the zazen we do, so this zazen is called Buddha's zazen.

The sixteen-foot golden figure is Buddha. Buddha is the person who swims on the surface of the ocean with a foot touching the bottom of the ocean. This is a huge person; don't you think so? If we swim just on the surface, we are tiny. But if we touch the bottom, we are huge—we are Buddha! Then, at the pivot of nothingness, everything becomes wonderful, beautiful. This is the grandeur of Buddha's world. Dogen always emphasizes the importance of seeing that everyday life is nothing but "grandeur and radiant illumination" reflected in the beautiful mirror at the pivot of nothingness.

The words *twelve hours* express the usual stream of time, the idea of time we use in everyday life. The phrase "three heads and eight arms" implies particular beings. Whatever we can see, whatever we can hear, whatever we can think of, all are particular beings in the stream of time. We think that twelve hours is the time a clock shows, but watch out! We have to learn what the time we encounter now really is! When Buddha's world is seen in terms of its particular aspects, time is called everyday time, so the idea of time that we use in everyday life "cannot but be identical" with real time, no-time, or timelessness because our idea of time is a particular being that is manifested by real time at the pivot of nothingness.

We cannot see real time unless it is manifested as twelve hours of everyday life because real time is formless. It is formless because it is constantly moving. Real time is always with us, but we cannot know it objectively. In our daily lives we constantly touch real time, but we don't pay attention to it. Instead of paying attention we suffer and grumble. We cannot see ourselves straightforwardly because we are always judging and evaluating, feeling good or bad. This keeps us busy. Sometimes it gives us a headache.

If we do touch the zero of time, we cannot stand up there. We try to escape, crying and screaming; sometimes we go skiing or watch TV. We keep busy, constantly working, because we don't really understand how time functions. But the busier we are, the more we want to push ourselves, doing more and more, until finally we don't know how to take a breath. We become crazy, exhausted, or sick.

How can you take care of time before you go crazy? Try to realize that real time is nothing but dynamic function, so time itself possesses the great power to emancipate you from the limitations of your idea of time.

Our modern daily life is pretty busy, but can we always be busy? No, you cannot stay with twelve hours or you would go crazy. So busyness has the great power to emancipate itself. That's why you want to find a way to be free from busyness and just be present quietly. This is quietness, tranquillity. When you are calm, tranquil, and still, twelve hours of time returns to no-time or timelessness. Can you stay with quietness? No, quietness has the great power to act. You cannot stay with timelessness or you would die, so timelessness must become twelve hours again. At the pivot of nothingness, timelessness manifests as your daily life. This is busyness, dynamism. Busyness and quietness are always working together in your life. This is reality.

In everyday life there is tranquillity in dynamism and dynamism in tranquillity. You touch timelessness and your life is tranquil stillness. Then twelve hours come up and your life is dynamic action. Dogen Zenji says that you swim on the surface of the ocean and walk at the bottom of the ocean. It's impossible to understand this intellectually, but you can really do it. Actually you always do it; it's just that you don't realize it.

When you understand this, you can use twelve hours instead of being used by them. Right in the middle of the busyness of daily life, you can find tranquillity, because you know that your life is based on the quietness of timelessness. You need enough calmness or tranquillity to see the overall picture of our life. Then you can deal with daily life with a calm mind. But we have limitations, so sometimes you want to be in the wilderness where you can come back to timelessness exactly. Then you can return to work again.

QUESTIONING AND DOUBT

Next Dogen Zenji says: "Even though we do not measure the twelve hours as long or short, remote or urgent, we still call it twelve hours. The imprint of time's coming and going is so evident that we do not doubt it. Although we do not doubt it, we do not understand it. That sentient beings doubt what they do not understand is entirely unsettled. Because of that, their past doubts do not necessarily coincide with the present doubt. Yet doubt itself is nothing but time."

We really don't know whether the twelve hours of everyday life is long or short because we feel that the day drags on when we are bored, and a pleasant day is shorter than an insipid day. Yet we accept our understanding of time with no questions. Still, how many people are crazy and exhausted, or fighting with each other? There is no peace or harmony. So even though it seems that we understand twelve hours because we don't have any questions, we don't actually understand. We still believe that the past, present, and future exist separately, and we don't think that they are pictures drawn by our consciousness at the pivot of nothingness.

On the other hand, we have lots of questions in twelve hours. For example, we set up the schedule for a retreat and all you have to do is jump in and follow it. When it's time to have a meal, just eat. It's simple. But people have lots of questions: Why do we have to bow? Why do we have to use chopsticks? So there are many questions, but this questioning is very unsettled.

When we begin to study Buddhism, we don't have many questions because we realize how wonderful Buddhism is. Buddhism fascinates us. When I began practicing Buddhism, I was really happy because the world was blooming every day. It was wonderful! I didn't have time to make up questions. Then, the more deeply I entered practice, the more questions I had, because trying to understand Buddhism is just like grasping at clouds. Finally I had one big question: What is Buddhism? I thought, "Why did I become a monk? That was a big mistake. Should I go back to what I was? Is there any other occupation for me?" There were lots of things that I was interested in, but actually there was no other occupation that fit me. Even though I felt it was a big mistake, there was no other way to go. So I stayed with the old priest who was my teacher, but lots of unanswered questions always came up. Then I thought, "Why don't you teach me anything?" But my teacher didn't care. He just lived. He just let me be alive every day.

Imagine you have a question that no one will answer. You try to research the question, but you still don't get exactly the right answer. So you keep it warm in your heart every day and just live. In a month or so, do you still have that question? Sometimes you do. But sometimes, in the process of living, the question disappears because life itself gives you the answer. The question you had a month ago is not always the same a month later.

For instance, you may ask, "Why do we have to bow? Please tell me, otherwise I don't want to bow." But if you are practicing at a Zen center, reality compels you to bow. So you continue to bow. A year later, bowing is not an important question; it is just a bow. So where is your question, where is your doubt? Dogen Zenji says, "Doubt itself is nothing but time." This is a really deep understanding of doubt.

Sometimes we think doubt is not good, but doubt is important. It's not so important that we should become crazy from it, but if you are questioning, that's fine. We need to question. Even though you don't get answers to your questions, all you have to do is just swim. Questioning is always going on in real time; it is always returning to zero. So, little by little, questioning becomes questionlessness. That's why Dogen says to swim on the surface of the ocean with your foot touching the bottom of the ocean. This is just swimming. We have to swim in the big scale of the world. Then questioning is also right in the middle of time, and very naturally questions disappear. Why do they disappear? What makes them disappear? Time, truth, buddha-nature, makes them disappear. Time gives us questions; time gives us answers to our questions.

THE WAY-SEEKING MIND

Dogen Zenji continues: "The self arrays itself and forms the entire universe. Perceive each particular thing in this entire universe as a moment of time. Things do not hinder one another, just as moments do not hinder one another. For this reason, the whole world of time is arousing the way-seeking mind; the whole world of the mind is arousing time. The same is true with practice and attaining the way. Thus, the self sets the self out in array and sees itself. This is the understanding that self is time."

Now Dogen brings up the idea of self, that is, a person. Before this he said that time must be understood in close, interconnected relationship with all sentient beings because time is not only time, it is also being. He also said that being-time is not the imaginary world of the past, present, and future that is fabricated by our consciousness. But this is not clear enough. We still don't understand time. How does time turn into being, or into grandeur and illumination? Who causes this to happen? We do! We can make time alive in our personal lives. Then time is not abstract; it is real, and it helps and influences daily life.

How can we make time alive in our lives? Usually we set ourselves out in a small territory of life, understand it, and then we feel good. So we want to hang on to that small territory. But this is not the way to make time alive. Whether we like it or not, time is constantly freeing us from our small territory. For example, children in the first grade are freed from the first grade, and the next year they enter second grade. The second grade doesn't keep children, so next year it's the third grade. When we realize that time gives everything the great power to emancipate itself from itself, then step-by-step we can make our lives mature. Instead of hanging on to our territory, we can use time to constantly develop and deepen our lives.

Time in "the whole world of time" is not usual time; it is timelessness, being, or freedom. My translation, "the whole world of time is arousing the way-seeking mind," is not wrong, but it is too free a translation. In the original Japanese, Dogen made just one word: *do-ji-hos-shin*. Literally it is translated as "the same-and-one-time-arousing-mind."

The same-and-one-time represents time as timelessness. Arousing-mind represents time in the realm of the twelve-hour world. Mind means heart, in other words: buddha-mind, buddha-nature, or the way-seeking mind. Whatever you say—mind, practice, enlightenment, or nirvana—all is the human world. Saying timelessness is simultaneously arousing mind means that timelessness is the whole world of your life: timelessness is exactly the twelve-hour human world, and the human world is exactly timelessness. Dogen's one word expresses this understanding.

But there is still a dualistic sense there, so next Dogen

says, "the same-and-one-mind-arousing-time." My translation is "the whole world of the mind is arousing time." Time in "arousing time" is timelessness. Mind in "the same-and-one-mind" means the twelve-hour human world. In a dualistic sense, twelve hours are separate and cannot be combined, but here Dogen says "the same-and-one-mind." That is Buddha's mind.

Mind arousing time means, when conditions are arranged and the time is ripe, timelessness appears. At that time, forms appear as formlessness: trees are treelessness, Katagiri is Katagiri-lessness, and zazen is zazenlessness. Real time comes up with no gap, and zazen is a wonderful being creating cushions, people sitting next to each other, the sound of the cars, all completely as one. Twelve-hour time never leaves its own trace; it just becomes timelessness. That is arousing time.

Arousing means simultaneity with no dualism. It's pretty hard to express the meaning of simultaneity in a word. If you can find a word to express it, that is wonderful, but I cannot do it. That's why Dogen Zenji says, "the same-and-one-time-arousing-mind, the same-and-one-mind-arousing-time." When you put Dogen's words together, it means that time is exactly timelessness and simultaneously mind. Timelessness is arousing mind, and mind is arousing timelessness. There is no gap, no separation. When I try to explain simultaneity, my explanation is still just an idea created by the time process. But practically speaking, if you practice zazen exactly, you are right in the middle of simultaneity.

If you set yourself out in Buddha's world and practice zazen, the way-seeking mind, *bodhi*-mind, appears. This is mind arousing time as zazen. In the next moment you hate zazen and want to go back to sleep, so the way-seeking mind disappears. Where does it go? It disappears in timelessness. Later you want to do zazen again. That is time arousing mind as religious aspiration. So you sit down and come back to practicing zazen. Then the way-seeking mind comes up again. All you have to do is continue arousing the way-seeking mind. If you practice like this, this is arousing time as zazen. So do zazen as whole-hearted practice and become completely one with time as zazen. Then time takes care of your life.

The way-seeking mind is not something you try to get. You just set yourself out in Buddha's world and do zazen wholeheartedly. When the time is ripe and conditions are arranged, the way-seeking mind comes up in your life, blooms, and is the rhythm of the whole world. Then time is called zazen and zazen is the whole world of time.

The whole world comes together into your zazen, but it doesn't bother your zazen. The sound of a car doesn't bother you, the sound becomes one with zazen. People sitting next to you don't bother you. Zazen doesn't bother you, and your zazen doesn't bother others. You just sit, blooming your life. This is called satori, enlightenment.

Setting "the self out in array" in Buddha's world is egolessness. At the pivot of nothingness, egolessness all at once creates the whole world of trees, birds, and all things. It is just like pushing a tiny button on a television set and creating a huge world. You become one with time, and simultaneously you form the entire world. Then the provisional world of daily life becomes the wonderful, grand, and radiantly illuminated world of enlightenment.

Practicing zazen and attaining enlightenment, you feel the beauty of existence. Whatever you see, you feel this beauty. It's very hard to express this in words, but through experience you can understand it. The same practice applies to daily life. If we want to have relaxation and security in our daily existence, we have to live wholeheartedly like this. This is a simple life.

What we call the conscious world is nothing but a provisional picture of the world produced by our dualistic human minds. Is there anything wrong with our provisional pictures? I don't think so. If we think the world is just something imaginary or provisional, it appears to have no value and we become pessimistic. But remember, the conscious world is also time; our provisional pictures are beings in Buddha's world. So why don't you accept them that way and deal with them as Buddha? Try to see the provisional world reflected in the big mirror of reality, not your egoistic telescope.

For example, when you use the toilet, you don't believe it's a provisional picture in an imaginary world, because you can see the toilet right in front of you. But the toilet you see is a toilet fabricated by your consciousness. The real toilet is just like time—every moment it goes away. All you have to do is just use it, just handle the toilet as Buddha, and live with the toilet in peace and harmony. This is everyday practice.

Whatever task you have in the provisional world, even though you don't want to do it, sometimes you have to do it. So perceive and accept yourself in Buddha's world.

For example, if you are asked to serve as the abbot of a Zen center after you are mature, when you look at yourself carefully you will see that even though people say you are mature, you are not. Maturity is an endless process. The time will never come when you reach your idea of maturity. So when people say you should be abbot, whether you feel qualified or not, all you have to do is accept it and do your best with wholeheartedness. Make every possible effort to meet this position with modesty and humility and just do it without being proud of yourself.

This is called setting the self out in array in Buddha's world. It means to constantly develop—sometimes in a positive way, sometimes in a modest way, sometimes in a passive way. The position of abbot is in a bigger scale than the person you believe yourself to be. So set yourself out in the big scale of the world. Before you're conscious of it, your life is deepened by the position. In that way you develop very naturally and become abbot of the Zen center.

Whoever you are, the whole world gives you energy to be free from what you think your capabilities are, from the form of a lifestyle, from the form of Zen or any teaching, whatever it is. Time is constantly giving you energy to emancipate yourself from any form or idea, even though you want to hold on to it. How can we accept time like this? Try to realize that you have already set yourself out in the vastness of the Buddha's world because you exist as a human being. So all you can do now is make every possible effort to live in Buddha's world with a way-seeking mind.

Usually we don't want to do this. If we step outside the familiar patterns of our lives we are scared. But we have to do it sometimes, so we should do it positively. This is very important for us. If we do it positively, we realize how great our capability is. That doesn't mean to become strong by expressing our ego. Expressing the ego seems to make us strong, but it is the complete opposite. In Zen monasteries the ego is always being hit on the head, like pouring water over a burning fire. Immediately *pffft*! Nothing is left. It's pretty hard, but this is the way to become strong.

Human beings have big, egoistic, balloon heads, so Dogen Zenji is always puncturing them, one by one, making a little hole and letting the air come out. Finally a balloon pops and you say, "Ah, I understand." But by that time maybe it's too late; maybe you understand right before you have one foot in the grave. That's why Dogen teaches us how to accept time as being and how our life can be illuminated right now.

INTIMACY WITH ALL BEINGS

At the end of the passage we are studying, Dogen Zenji says:

> Know that in this way there are myriads of forms
> and hundreds of grasses in the entire earth, and yet
> each grass and each form itself is in the entire earth.
> The process of this kind is the beginning of practice.
> When you reach this state, you are one grass, one
> form; you have understanding of form and no un-
> derstanding of form; you have understanding of

grass and no understanding of grass. Because there is only this time, being-time is entire time. This being-grass, this being-form, both are time. At each and every moment, there are myriad beings. They are the entire universe. Reflect now whether any myriad beings or any entire universe is left out of time in nowness.

Before this, Dogen said that the self arrays itself and forms the entire universe, so saying "in this way" here means first of all we have to set ourselves out in array in Buddha's world to form the entire world. That is egolessness. Usually we don't do this. We set ourselves out in our own small territory called "I" and see everything separately. We may use words like *close relationship* and *intimacy,* but we understand them intellectually; we don't understand real intimacy. Intimacy doesn't penetrate our skin, muscle, and bone, so we still live as if everything were separate.

We are happy in our small world, just like a frog in an old pond. But no one knows when a flood will come and carry the frog away. When that happens we are confused, and we don't know what to do. That's why we should learn what it means to set ourselves out in Buddha's world. In the human world we see other beings as separate from us. In Buddha's world all things come together and melt into one. So, very naturally, if we set ourselves out in array in Buddha's world, we can see all other beings. Then we know that we must live with others in peace and harmony because we are all intimately related, with no gap between. This is Buddha's world.

Buddha's world is a sort of fantastic fertilizer. If I say fertilizer, maybe you think, "I will give the grasses fertilizer so they will grow." That is dualistic because you are thinking that giving fertilizer and grass growing are separate. But they're not separate. The fertilizer is not something separate from the growth of grass; the fertilizer is simultaneously the growth of grass. In the same way, Buddha's world exists simultaneously with the human world. Otherwise the human world doesn't exist. In the huge universe, they are exactly one. That is great—a superfertilizer! This is the point we don't understand, but this is really true. This is called intimacy, the same-and-one, or absolute reality. Sometimes we call it freedom.

The statement "each grass and each form itself is in the entire earth" means that a particular form does not occupy a portion of the earth—it occupies the entire earth. When you set yourself out in array in Buddha's world, you are forming the whole world. If you only see yourself from your narrow view of time, you don't understand it, but this is true. This is walking at the bottom of the ocean. If we touch this point, even slightly, we see that all sentient beings are connected with us and we are connected with all sentient beings. We are connected, and simultaneously we are going back and forth. It's not exactly going back and forth, it's coming and going at superspeed. This is the real state of existence of all sentient beings.

When we realize this, it is called spiritual security. This is real security, called faith. Then we cannot be inactive; something compels us and we want to do something. That is called *bodhi*-mind. It is the way-seeking mind of spiritual aspiration, which comes up when we realize that myriad beings exist together in the entire earth and are not separate from us. When we see that grasses, tables, ourselves, and other people are not separate, then, very naturally, we want to do something with all sentient beings. This spiritual aspiration is manifested in action called practice. *Bodhi*-mind appears and simultaneously turns into practice.

When you practice with all sentient beings, it is the beginning of real practice. Real practice is done simultaneously in the realm of the twelve hours of daily life and the realm of timelessness. You act on the surface of the ocean, and your action is stable, walking firmly at the bottom of the ocean. This is called *bodhi*. When you and your practice are stable in this process, all sentient beings come together and you are one stable being, walking at the bottom of the ocean and swimming on the surface of the ocean.

When all sentient beings come together, Buddha Shakyamuni, Bodhidharma, Dogen, and all of us are in the same place, which is called the entire earth. All are interconnected, closely and intimately related. That means Buddha is not something separate or far from here. Buddha is you. That's why you become Buddha. You are Buddha, Bodhidharma, and Dogen simultaneously. At that time you can transmit your spirit to the next generation. This is not your spirit; this is *bodhi*-mind's spirit, Buddha Shakyamuni's spirit.

When you do zazen with all sentient beings, this is to save all sentient beings. To save all beings is your practice. But all beings are not something separate from you.

It's not "I save." This is intimacy. Sitting in zazen, practicing with all sentient beings, you become Buddha. At the same time, your activity becomes enlightenment. Carry this practice as long as possible, moment by moment and day by day, and this is called nirvana.

Then you say, "Oh, wonderful! I understand!" So you do zazen, concentrating on your breath, and you feel good. Maybe you think, "I am the entire world!" But wait a minute! That is a dualistic understanding. If you think practice is just for you to deepen your life, it is egoistic practice, not real practice. You understand something, but there are still myriad beings you don't understand.

When I was at Eiheiji monastery, my life was really perfect because all the 120 monks practiced according to a schedule. We got up at 2:00 A.M. and went to zazen. Even though we felt sleepy, we just went to practice. There was nothing to bother me, and every day my life was just like organic energy, going perfectly.

But after three years I went back to my small temple. Immediately my situation was completely different. My temple was at the foot of the mountains, far from the village. Just a cat and the old priest were there. I had to do many things: wash clothes, fix the meals, doing everything by myself. It was completely opposite from life in the monastery. My life became very busy, just like a business. There was always something to do. Time was haunting me. Everyday life was always haunting me, and I was very confused. So even though I understood zazen in the monastery, it was not good enough. There were still lots of things I didn't know.

Even though we understand who we are, we have to see what we are. Are we separate from the grasses, trees, or birds? No, we *are* grasses and trees, snowstorms and fine days. So we have to learn what the storm is, what winter is, what spring is. We have to understand everything in our whole life. So accept that life is just a continuation of learning. Day after day, life after life, we just have to learn constantly. That's enough.

Finally, if you set yourself out in Buddha's world and see other beings intimately, you see that the unity of being and time is the entire world. Grass is being, so each grass is the entire world, you are the entire world, and the whole world is the entire world. Nothing is left out; nothing is wasted. Then you can live with all sentient beings in peace and harmony.

16   TOTAL DYNAMIC WORKING

Dogen Zenji constantly encourages us to go beyond our usual understanding of time and see real time. What is real time? Real time is seen as the harmony of twelve hours of everyday life and the source of twelve hours called timelessness. The word *harmony* means time is the activity of every moment.

I always say the original nature of existence is a kind of energy or total dynamic working. When I say this, you may think that I'm talking about a constant motion, but that is not what I mean. Dogen uses the word *circulation*. He says, "Being-time has the virtuous quality of circulation." If you hear the word *circulation,* you immediately think of something moving from one place to another. It seems to be dualistic. But time is not like that. Circulation is motion and no-motion. It is dynamism in stillness, stillness in dynamism.

Stillness means eternal time, timelessness. When time does not have the characteristic of coming and going, time doesn't move; it's very quiet. All sentient beings are interconnected, and there is no fixed individual being. This is called being, or no-time. On the other hand, dynamism means being-time. When time does have the characteristic of coming and going, time moves but there is no distance. There is no gap between stillness and dynamism. All sentient beings are interconnected in the huge universe and all at once the whole universe moves. *Pop!* The world of being-time appears.

You and I and all sentient beings are eternal time that is very still, and we are also being-time that is dynamically moving from moment to moment. If you see time that doesn't have the characteristic of coming and going, you are stable and quiet. If you see time that does have the characteristic of coming and going, you exist here and now in being-time.

When you are eternal time, you are not the ordinary you that you usually believe yourself to be, you are the big you that exists in the entire world. You have to depend on the big you. If you do that, you have spiritual security. If you ignore this, you are always depending on something else. You may live peacefully for a certain period of time, but you never know how long you can depend on other things. Maybe there will be a flood or a chemical bomb that destroys what you are depending on. So whatever happens, you have to depend on the big you. You can depend on your self because eternal time is always with you. And because eternal time is always with you, when you practice, it will come up and you can realize it.

What is practice? Practice is to manifest the object of your activity—zazen, cooking, sports, or whatever you are doing—as a being that exists in eternal time. If you do something wholeheartedly, all sentient beings come into your life. Then if you look at a table, you see the table as a beautiful being that exists with you right now, right here. This is called oneness.

Usually you see the world through your egoistic telescope, so you believe your life is separate from a table's life. But if you think that way, you cannot see the table as it really is. You may not care about the life of the table; you may break it up and use it as firewood. Seeing the table only through your narrow egoistic view is killing the life of the table.

The Buddhist precept that tells you not to kill doesn't just mean not to physically kill people or animals. If you deeply understand the meaning of the precept no killing life, you know that not killing the life of the table means not handling the table according to an egoistic view that separates you from the table. No killing life means see the table as it really is and handle the table as a manifestation of eternal time, where there is no gap between subject and object. This is to animate the life of the table as Buddha.

How can you do this? As much as possible, try to handle the table as something more than an object in the realm of twelve hours. Handle the table wholeheartedly, with compassion and kindness. At that time practice comes up very naturally, just like water from an underground spring, and this practice deepens and develops your life.

So, to understand Dogen's word *circulation*, the first point is that we have to practice, and then, right in the process of practice, the huge universe moves and a magnanimous world comes up. *Pop!* Here is *gassho!* All sentient beings are set out in array in the universe at the pivot of time and space, and you bow. Then *gassho* appears as being-time, or maybe it is called *gassho*-time: the actualization of all sentient beings appearing as a form of bowing that can be seen in the stream of twelve hours but is coming up from eternal time. When you make this *gassho,* your bow manifests itself as eternal time and is really stable. You are dynamically moving and also very still. Your bow swims on the surface of the ocean and walks at the bottom of the ocean. That is enlightenment. At that time you are buddha-nature.

The second point is that to practice is to manifest eternal time right in the middle of being-time. It means to be master of yourself in whatever situation you may be. When you practice zazen as buddha-nature, this is real zazen: eternal time is connected with all sentient beings, and your practice doesn't manifest only the small you; it manifests the big you, the self that is the whole universe. You become one with zazen, and simultaneously your zazen influences others. Even when you don't intend to influence anyone, your activity always influences others because your life is interconnected with the life of all sentient beings. That's why we cannot just take care of our own lives and ignore others' lives. To live in peace and harmony, we have to understand the total dynamic working of time and think about what it means to say that our life always influences others' lives.

17 DELUSION AND SUFFERING

Everyday life is an opportunity, a place where we can return to oneness and manifest eternal time, but this is a big project for us. Day by day we have to go into the mud of delusion in order to manifest eternal time. Delusion means we go astray from the purity of oneness and see beings in terms of separation. According to Dogen Zenji's term, this is called going into mud and water.

Going astray doesn't seem to be good, but actually we have to go astray, because in daily life we live in the world of twelve hours. In eternal time, a table is not something separate from your life. But in daily life, you have to pay attention to the table as a separate being in order to figure out the best way to deal with the table without killing the life of the table. Then you experience the pain of being separate from the table, and you suffer from it.

In my case, in order to deal with giving talks, I must constantly go astray from oneness. Sometimes it makes my head ache when I have to give talks. Sometimes I want to stop. But there is no way I can stop. I have to think how to explain Buddhism, how to say what I want to say. I have to use words, but my words are separate from the truth, so I suffer. But where is my suffering located? The whole universe! I cannot escape from twelve hours of everyday life, but I also cannot ignore the fact that twelve hours is something more than daily life. Twelve hours is delusion, and also a being that exists in the universe. Mud and water are just time, so in mud and water there is always an opportunity to live in peace and harmony.

The point of Buddhist practice is to act. There is always an opportunity to live in peace and harmony, but we have to do something right now! If we do something wholeheartedly, all sentient beings come together and support our lives. When you see daily life and eternal time simultaneously, suffering disappears.

I became a monk when I was eighteen years old. In the process of getting to where I am now, I have experienced many ups and downs. But this up-and-down life really helps me and teaches me who Katagiri is, what zazen is, what Buddha's teaching is. For me there is no escape from giving talks, sitting zazen, or attending a *sesshin* (intensive meditation retreat), so I just do it. Maybe I should hate *sesshin* because of the schedule, but in my heart I enjoy zazen. I understand zazen and say that I will do zazen forever, life after life. That's my feeling now.

If we take care of whatever we do with wholeheartedness and devote ourselves to dealing with our lives as a monk, housewife, painter, carpenter, or philosopher, we cannot stop. We don't want to stop, because we really enjoy it. We want to do it forever. This is continuous development: you constantly deepen your life. If you practice like this, you attain enlightenment. At that time, whatever you do, you are stable. That is spiritual security.

Dogen has another interesting way of presenting the nature of suffering. He says, "The past swallows up the present and spits it out." It's impossible to understand this intellectually, but it means reflecting on yourself. That is dualist human consciousness. When you reflect on yourself, the past swallows up the present. Then suffering appears in your life because, through reflecting, you go astray from oneness and suffer from delusion.

But then something happens: the past spits out the present. This means gratitude; the past is alive in the present as gratitude because suffering is great fertilizer. When we reflect on ourselves and suffer, we can realize that we are deluded, repent, and return to oneness. If you break the bottom of suffering, you laugh. Nothing can imitate this—not animals, birds, or trees—nothing! Only humans become great laughter through suffering.

When we return to oneness and realize that all lives are the same as ours, we cannot sit in our own small territory; we start to move and share our life with people because we really appreciate our lives. All at once the past swallows up the present and spits it out. *Pop!* At the pivot of nothingness the next moment unfolds and a new world appears. This is the total dynamic working of time, the process of eternal development.

Dogen also says, "The present swallows up the past." It means that when you are buddha-nature, you are just in the present. The past, the present, and the future are beings, but they are interconnected right now. So the past is not something separate from the present; the past is exactly the same as the present. Then eternity is alive in everyday life. That is real enlightenment. How do we make eternity alive in our lives? With our wisdom we can do it. To place yourself in the harmony of time and timelessness is to practice; being in the harmony of twelve hours and timelessness is enlightenment.

18   PRACTICE AND ENLIGHTENMENT

Our usual understanding of enlightenment is that if we practice zazen, we will become an enlightened person as a result. We think of enlightenment as a doorway to reach a goal: reach nirvana as soon as possible in order to satisfy human curiosity and desire. But that can make us very short-tempered. We cannot live in peace, with a feeling of security. We don't know how, because we don't base our lives on direct experience of real peace. This is a human problem.

Enlightenment is a state in which we are exactly one with the truth and see the ultimate nature of existence. When you really see time, you are present from moment to moment and a huge magnanimous world comes up. Whether you have experienced this or not, whether you are conscious of it or not, you already exist right in the middle of this magnanimous world. You are already an enlightened person because you are alive; you exist at the intersection of time and space. Your intellectual understanding cannot penetrate this, but through spiritual practice you can see it. When you see the original face of a moment, it is exactly nothing, but that nothing is very strong and vigorous, very active and energetic. Even though you don't know that this is life, it is why you survive. It makes you vividly alive.

The opportunity to live is something vigorous, just like a leaping fish. That leaping fish is eternity. Is eternity something that exists forever? Yes, but eternity is not something fixed or absolute. Eternity is leaping and alive, constantly changing. We cannot pin down exactly what it is, but we are alive because something supports our life and helps us live—something that exists always. This is called eternity, or the absolute.

Human beings are originally peaceful and harmonious because eternity is alive in our daily life. It is not a matter of metaphysical, philosophical, psychological, or religious understanding; it is fact. But we don't realize this because we stumble over our feelings, emotions, and ideas. When we see human life only in terms of ordinary time, where everything is chopped into separate pieces, then our eyes aren't open to see life in terms of universal time, where we are interconnected and interpenetrated with all sentient beings. So whatever we do in daily life, we have to make every possible effort to do it in peace and harmony with all beings.

When your daily living becomes one with peace and harmony, all beings are absorbed into your life and you become one with the original nature of existence. This is the manifestation of real peace. If you haven't experienced this, is seems to be abstract. But it's not abstract. There is nothing to conceptualize.

Zazen is an opportunity to let go of conceptualized thought. When you sit down, let go of yourself and be free from the idea that you are someone who is doing zazen. Then you are fluid and dynamic. When you practice like this, your zazen arouses the way-seeking mind, and at the same time the way-seeking mind causes you to practice. Practice is like a filter: on one side is everyday life, and on the other side is direct experience of reality. This filter is not merely a device—it must be functioning. Something must be going through it. This is not a matter of discussion; we must be alive! We must act! Then zazen passes through the filter of practice, and in the next moment enlightenment appears.

Through our spiritual practice we experience wisdom, deeply seeing the truth of human life. Seeing eternity, dharma, truth, or the source of existence is complete freedom. Then, when everyday life is based on wisdom, it is called nirvana. The way-seeking mind, practice, enlightenment, and nirvana are constantly going in a circle that is beginningless and endless. They are nothing but being, nothing but time; this is called being-time. Being-time is a great device through which we can glance at the real self and come back to human life.

Enlightenment is not a particular state of mind that you perceive from a dualistic perspective; it is not something to try to get, something to be infatuated with, or something to stay with. We have to realize it, but enlightenment is beyond dualistic human perception. It is seeing life from the universal perspective. We live in peace and harmony with all sentient beings without discrimination. So instead of expecting something from zazen, just do zazen with wholeheartedness. Then you can see the entire universe. That is egolessness. At that time zazen is seen from eternity, and the zazen you do is manifested with the whole universe. This is real time, and this time is called enlightenment.

When egolessness comes up simultaneously with practice, practice is free from suffering. You become free from your own body and mind and experience complete spiritual security, stability, and imperturbability. This is called emancipation. Emancipation—the individual, direct experience of human life—is the culmination of the quest. Sometimes we say this is realization, or actualization. Actualization is not just the manifestation of your individual experience of the truth; it is your life interconnected with a tree's life, a bird's life, water's life, spring's life, autumn's life, and the life of the whole universe.

Buddhism teaches that all things—those we can see and those we cannot see, those we can think of and those we cannot think of, those we can imagine and those we cannot imagine—must be accepted as beings in Buddha's world. We should accept all beings and understand them: see where they come from, look at their face; and at the same time we should be free from all things. So just accept all aspects of human life, whatever they are. This is called freedom. Freedom is not escape from suffering or any of the various aspects of human life but acceptance of their true nature as beings in Buddha's world.

19   LIVING IN REAL TIME

Even though we don't have any proof, we can sense there is a beautiful world that can be seen with something more than our intellectual understanding. Seeing the vast expanse of human life is a target you can aim at—a destination. But you shouldn't be crazy about reaching it, because everyday life is already right now, right here. Right now, right here is the present moment—time.

Dogen Zenji tells us that even though we believe there is only the system of time that measures twenty-four hours in a day, this is not a complete understanding of time. Real time is the harmony of the time process—past, present, and future—with the source of time: timelessness.

If you haven't experienced timelessness, when Dogen describes it as the immense expanse of space where all sentient beings are interconnected in peace and harmony, it seems to be an abstract, metaphysical understanding. You can accept it that way, but a metaphysical view shouldn't be just metaphysical. Dogen's metaphysical understanding comes from his deep insight and empirical research for many, many years. So why don't you understand the metaphysical aspect of human life and investigate how to make it alive in your everyday life? This is what Dogen really emphasizes.

How can we practice the harmony of time and timelessness in everyday life? Dogen says just swim in the ocean that reflects all sentient beings. Who swims? Each one of us swims. It's not an idea; our whole body and mind swims in this entire world. That's wonderful! How do we swim? We swim on the surface and simultaneously walk at the bottom of the ocean. This is a fantastic explanation. It's beautiful. But we don't understand it. So Dogen always explains this in a concrete way. In *Shobogenzo* there is a particular chapter on washing your face, and another on cleaning your room, the toilet, and so on. These are concrete examples of how we can practice swimming in the entire ocean. This is our practice. We can do it! Dogen constantly emphasizes that practice is *shikan*. *Shikan* is just wholeheartedness; it is experience, so practice is experience.

Practice as experience is based on the manifestation of reality. Manifestation means the relationship between subject and object. We manifest subject and object in many ways through the six consciousnesses of sight, sound, smell, taste, touch, and thought. So we can manifest practice with our mind. But practicing just with the mind is not good enough; we also have to practice with our body.

For example, when you are cooking and you use a vegetable, if you think, "This is a vegetable," it immediately becomes an object, something that is separate from you, and you see the vegetable in the ordinary way. But you can take a different attitude toward the vegetable. Before you consciously label the vegetable, you can touch and handle the vegetable as something more than a vegetable—Buddha—and face the vegetable in terms of time-lessness with no label. This is really the attitude we should take. This is wisdom. Then cooking is practice based on manifesting reality.

This is a very difficult practice, but with wisdom you can face the real vegetable, which is not something separate from you. Then even though your dualistic consciousness says, "Oh, that is a vegetable," wisdom keeps you straight. So calm your dualistic consciousness and just face the vegetable. Place the vegetable right in the middle of timelessness. When you place your object, the vegetable, in the middle of timelessness, then your subject, you, is also placed in the middle of timelessness. At that time, all things come back to nothingness, emptiness, and you wake up.

But practically speaking, you cannot ignore the fact that you and the vegetable exist in everyday life. So how should you deal with a vegetable? First place the vegetable in timelessness, where carrots, cabbage, and potatoes all exist with no discrimination. Then come back to everyday time, where you cannot cut a carrot the same way you cut a potato, because a carrot is a being with its own characteristics. Recognize that the carrot is a carrot and deal with your carrot without confusing it with potatoes, water, or the pan. When you deal with a carrot like this, you manifest yourself as a cook and the carrot as a particular being, but at the same time both you and the carrot are manifested as Buddha.

If you take this wholehearted attitude toward the carrot, the carrot blooms and you bloom. The carrot and you are walking at the bottom of the ocean, where all beings are interconnected, and there is no gap between the carrot and you. This means you are emancipated from the form of you and from the form of your carrot. That is called enlightenment. At that time you cannot think, you just have to be there. To "just be there" means to completely open your heart. Then, in a moment, you can see something. Everything turns over, and the whole situation becomes beautiful.

If you haven't experienced this, that's okay. Never mind. Sometimes it happens. But it's difficult to realize this experience, because the circumstances of our daily lives are very complicated, and human consciousness is very picky, always picking up something to examine. It's impossible for our consciousness to believe that a carrot can become one with a person, so we immediately think of "carrot" and "I" separately. So should we try to throw away our human consciousness? No, we cannot do it. But what we can do is constantly, wholeheartedly, just place "carrot" and "I" in timelessness. This is our practice.

No matter what our consciousness tells us, we should handle the carrot with compassion and just place the carrot in timelessness, as simply as we can. At that time we are placing ourselves in timelessness. We come to the carrot and simultaneously the carrot comes to us, and we come together with no gap. This is called manifesting buddha-nature. At that time, the reality of the phenomenal world is absorbed into the reality of Buddha's world. When we manifest our self and our object like this, we experience total reality. This is called freedom, emancipation. Emancipation has no particular characteristics, it is just action.

But what if you don't understand real time; can you still live freely in peace and harmony? Yes, you can! Even if you don't understand real time through a teacher's explanation or your own practice, you, the carrot, the pan, and the water already exist in the big ocean. Everything is there. There are no exceptions! Misunderstanding is also in the big ocean. Misunderstanding cannot exist separately from understanding, so understanding is there too, whether you believe it or not.

Misunderstanding is like a potato being washed in a big bamboo basket. When I was at my temple in Japan, we put potatoes in a bamboo basket and put the basket in a small creek. The water would run through the basket just like a mill, rolling the potatoes inside until they were very clean. That was an organic machine! Misunderstandings or mistakes are just potatoes in the big ocean. So accept mistakes exactly the same way you accept pleasure and happiness. A mistake is a mistake, so handle mistakes in twelve hours without mixing them up with happiness. But also put both the mistake and you in the realm of timelessness. Sooner or later a beautiful potato comes up. This is Buddha's compassion.

Buddha is always sharing compassion with all sentient beings. Even though we stumble, stumbling is also in the same ocean. Even if we don't have hope for the future and think our life is a mistake, still we are wandering in Buddha's world. Dogen says that Buddha's door is constantly open to everybody. So why don't we live wholeheartedly, taking care of our everyday life, listening to Buddha's teaching, constantly trying to follow the Buddha's way. Then maybe we can make our potato clean in a shorter time.

Everyday life is very important. It gives you data about how vast your life is. You can't ignore daily life, but you can't ignore the destination either. So the center of your boat should be directed toward your destination. Your boat should be stable and calm, taking one step, and then another step, in whatever circumstances you are. That is wholeheartedness. Wholeheartedness is a very simple practice that gives you lots of information about how to take care of everyday life. Then everyday life carries you to the destination.

Even though we don't understand, we have to practice like this. Someday a wonderful hope will come up. If we don't practice, I don't know how long it will take, because the water is not always streaming. Sometimes the water is still and the potato stops rolling. We don't know what will happen. So continue practicing at any cost, even though you don't understand, even though you don't have an enlightenment experience like thunder and lightning. Most people believe awakening is like thunder and lightning. I don't think so. Awaking is very soft and gentle. Real enlightenment is awakening to where we are, who we are, what everyday life is, what time is.

We have to practice and deepen our understanding of time, but we cannot ignore everyday life. Even if you don't completely understand time, the human world, or your human life, still you have to take care of your life and others' lives every day. How do you live in peace?

First of all, understand how life arises and accept your life as being at the pivot of nothingness. Accept that within this pivot the human world is a picture you create. Then you can use time; you can use your human consciousness and choose what to do. You create your life, which is interconnected with the life of all sentient beings, by your actions at the pivot of nothingness. This is the significant meaning of time in Buddhism.

PART FOUR

THE PRACTICE OF CREATIVE ACTION

Zen is a practice of action. Sometimes people think that Zen practice is a bridge between suffering and happiness: we practice first and then we will be happy. But practice and happiness are not separate. Practice is not a bridge—practice itself is joy. If you practice Buddha's Eightfold Noble Path of right seeing, thought, speech, conduct, livelihood, effort, mindfulness, and concentration completely, there is egolessness within your practice. Practicing egolessness doesn't mean that you destroy yourself and then something changes in the future. It means that egolessness comes up simultaneously with the activity of practice itself, and that practice is free from suffering.

Entering Buddha's path is arousing *bodhi*-mind. *Bodhi*-mind is translated as the way-mind or way-seeking mind. It means that Buddha's mind is the way, the right path to be walked, extending in all directions, continuously open to everybody. The word *right* isn't based on an idea of right and wrong, good and bad. Right means the complete, perfect harmony of the phenomenal world of time, which we create from moment to moment, and the source of existence, the eternal world of timelessness, where all sentient beings are always interconnected in peace and harmony. Right activity is the actualization of the phenomenal world and the source of existence coming together and working together.

When you fully devote yourself to your activity, the moment and you come together, creating a kind of momentum or energy. You and your activity become one, and this refined activity very naturally leads you to forget yourself. In a moment you go beyond the phenomenal world of time and space to the source of time, where your life is calm and stable and your activity is clear and pure. When there is no self-consciousness it is called *bodhi,* enlightenment. *Bodhi*-mind is freedom. It is the function of mind that is beyond dualistic consciousness. But to arouse *bodhi*-mind we have to use our discriminating, human mind. In other words, Buddha's mind is beyond human consciousness, but the only way to find out what it is is through conscious activity. That is why we practice.

In *Shobogenzo,* "Zazenshin" (Lancet of Seated Meditation), Dogen Zenji presents zazen as the practice of realizing *bodhi*-mind. But Dogen wants us to understand, very clearly, that practice is not a means to an end. Doing meditation, or any spiritual practice, because we want to be something special in the future is not the point of Zen practice. The point is to be free where we are now. Where we are is a problem, but where we are is also the beauty of existence. In Buddhism there are lots of psychological and philosophical analyses of the self because we have to learn where we are, who we are, and what a human being is. But to see the truth directly we have to practice.

Through practice we can be free from where we think we are, which lets us return to where we really are and experience what the self really is. Then we have to come back and help others. This is Buddhism.

20   BEST TIME, BEST PLACE, BEST PERSON

When you practice Buddhism, particularly when you do zazen, there are three important points: the time, the place, and the person. First, the time: what is the best time to do zazen? Is it a quiet time, a busy time, or a neutral time? Well, what is the best time to read a book? When you feel good? Maybe. When you read a book at the best time, sometimes the meaning of a sentence touches your heart. But sometimes you don't understand the sentence at all, because your mind has gone somewhere. So, what is the best time to read a book, what is the best time to do zazen? This question is important for us. The moment that something happens is very important.

For example, if you leave the city and go to the country, sometimes you see a deer, right in front of you. You are very surprised! You can get a big shock. The moment when the deer appears, you immediately forget who you are. You jump into that time and are completely absorbed into that moment. That time is very clear. The deer occupies the whole world, and you understand the real existence of the deer because you touch the deer's life. You are one with the deer, so you are silent. Then your consciousness starts to work. The deer becomes something you understand as a concept, so you say, "Wow, a deer!" But the real deer was understood at the exact moment when you met it and the deer appeared very clearly, like a moon.

That time is very important. That moment is very important. You see the real deer before your consciousness works and you say, "Deer!" In the same way, you can see zazen in a moment. What is that moment? Can you analyze that time as a concept? No, that moment is beyond analysis. But from moment to moment, you can see zazen occupying the whole world. So what is the best time to do zazen? Right now!

Place is also important. Let's imagine that we are sitting with each other on our cushions and we are talking. We are talking now, but before we started to talk we just sat down. We saw each other and mutually acknowledged each other's existence. At that time we created this place. If you want to say something about this place, maybe you say, "Hello!" Hello implies "right here" as the place where your existence and my existence are completely accepted and you and I communicate totally. I say, "Hello!" and then we start to talk about some topic. So after saying hello in the first moment, in the second moment we accept this as a place where discussion is possible. And then we can create a form of life called discussion.

Now imagine that you leave. You are not interested in talking about Buddhism, so you leave. Everyone leaves, and only the cushions you sat on are left. Should I continue to talk? It seems ridiculous, because I cannot maintain a conversation if no one else is here. But this place is important. Even if everyone leaves, I can continue to talk—I can talk with the cushions. At that time, these cushions are the basic place where the whole universe is reflected. In that place the cushions and I communicate with each other very naturally.

For you to have a time and place, it is necessary to be a person. A person is the unity of body and mind. But usually you are caught by the form of your body, and your mind becomes separate. For body to participate in mind, we have to practice concentration, full devotion. This is very important. When you fully devote yourself to your activity, your body becomes one with your consciousness, and you don't perceive the form of your body. For example, you watch a movie and someone in the movie cries. You know that it's just a movie, but before you're conscious of it, you start to cry too. Somebody may say you are stupid to cry when you see a movie, but it's not stupid—it's pretty good. It means you jumped into the activity on the screen and forgot the form of your own body.

So what is the best time, where is the best place, and who is the best person? The best person continues to talk with the cushions even if everyone leaves the room, because that person understands best time and best place. In terms of our usual sense, it's ridiculous. But at that time a person appears who understands the place where the whole universe can be seen and who can be present in oneness. That person sees the dualistic human world of empty cushions but is not disappointed, because the whole universe is there. That person can find the best time, the best place, and be the best person. It means to just be present in the universe and continue to talk about Buddha's world. You can do this! Right now, right here is the best time and place for you to do it, and you are a person who can practice this spiritual way of life.

21   THE FLOW OF THE RHYTHM OF LIFE

When I was a beginning driver, I drove to San Francisco on Route 101. That road is very curved. I tried to drive safely, but I was scared. My eyes were always on the road, pretty close to the car, and the dotted line really bothered me. The lines jumped out at me, like stars in my eyes, so my driving was very shaky. But if I looked away from the car, I also felt very unstable. So I didn't know what to do—where should I look? Finally I became exactly one with nature and just drove. Nature was always there, trying to help me, but in the beginning I was not ready to receive that help. So I continually tried to practice, and finally I could accept it. Nature came into me and was absorbed into my driving. Then my driving was safe.

When you are driving safely, your mind is never caught at a certain place. But if your mind is caught, you're confused, scared. That is just like our Zen practice. In the beginning we don't trust our practice. It's a little shaky. We don't know what to pay attention to: to ourselves, to zazen, to space? We know that we should accept the whole situation, but we don't know how. At that time all you can do is try to be present in this very moment. Unknown time and space is within that moment. All of nature is there, and myriad beings are walking together with you. So just continue to act with total devotion to what you are doing until there is total oneness between you and your activity. That is called *shikan,* or *samadhi.* You and nature melt into one.

If you are driving, you become one with driving. Your physical and mental forms are completely dissipated within the form of your car and the form of the situation. This is called full devotion to driving. At that time you don't perceive the form of your body, so your body and mind become one. That is called flexibility, or elasticity. You accept the whole situation before your consciousness starts to work, before your body starts to feel.

Acting with total wholehearted devotion, you know what you are doing, but your consciousness cannot touch action itself because your consciousness is dissipated within action. Then you can go beyond the frame of your body, beyond the perception of your mind, beyond the object of your activity, and see the perfect unity of your life with nature. If you play the piano, right in the middle of playing the piano, you can see that oneness. If you ski or climb mountains, you can see this.

Devote yourself to accomplishing something, and very naturally you experience no self-consciousness. At that time you really enjoy what you are doing. Then maybe you say it was fun. But what you enjoyed is not merely something that gives pleasure to you; there is something deep there. That is called enlightenment. If you are a skier, when you become one with your skis, the mountain, and the snow, you are just the practice of skiing. You are physical posture, mental posture, and breathing, and your activity is in perfect balance. There is no sense of self-consciousness, because you are really one with your skis and the mountain. You, your skis, the snow, and the mountain are all working together, and your activity is perfectly balanced, with no confusion.

If you experience skiing like this, you cannot stop doing it. When new snow falls, you immediately want to go skiing. People say it's dangerous and they criticize you. They ask you, "Why do you like such a dangerous sport?" But you don't care because you really enjoy your life with the mountain. You cannot stop, because when you and the mountain are in balance, there is peaceful feedback from your activity; some kind of momentum or energy is going between you and the mountain.

Who created this momentum? We don't know. Momentum is the autotelic nature of the moment, the nature of human activity itself. That's it! Activity has its own purpose within itself; there is no particular purpose external to itself. There is no reason to ski; you just really want to ski. You feel that something is compelling you, ordering you to be there. It's not that something actually compels you, but there is something that continually encourages you to ski. That is called flow—the flow of life.

When you ski, and nature and you melt into one, a mountain's life is not separate from your life. You look at the mountain, and the mountain melts into your body and mind and occupies the whole world. Through the mountain you feel the rhythm of life: You and the mountain are going in and out, the mountain is walking, the mountain is breathing. It's not someone's imagination—it's true. Through your life you can see the flow of universal life connected with a mountain's life, a river's life, or a tree's life. You are absorbed into nature, and you forget yourself.

I think everyone experiences oneness with activity. But it's very difficult to be there and maintain it, because we don't accept this comfortable situation with total confidence. Immediately we feel scared. Consciously or unconsciously, we want to return to the form of our body because this is our habit, the custom of our life. So we are caught by our habit and return to the human world. Then, even though we know what oneness is, it is far from us and we are always seeking a particular time and place where it can come close to us again: sports, skiing, music, art, dance, zazen, or parties. When you devote yourself to a party, you can completely forget yourself and experience oneness. You can do it gambling at Lake Tahoe. But there's a problem, because you are seeing oneness at a distance, in terms of human life.

The important point is, we must be in the flow of the rhythm of life first and then deal with human life. What is the flow of the rhythm of life? It is nothing but action. When you get up in the morning, how can you know the flow of the rhythm of life right in the middle of getting up? You have to participate in it. Then simultaneously you receive feedback. It's just like the computer that operates a ship. The computer gets information from the ship and simultaneously gives information to the ship— input and output. In order to do this, the computer can't stay with anything; it must be open and flexible. In the same way, when you get up in the morning, even though your consciousness is grumbling and making noise, your life must be flowing smoothly. You have to participate with full devotion. Then the universe gives you feedback, and you know how to behave properly in the realm of getting up in the morning.

But there is still a problem. You experience that perfect unity, that wonderful flexibility and elasticity, but you cannot totally accept it because you see oneness from a dualistic point of view, in terms of human life. If you want to practice spiritual life, you have to do the opposite; you have to see your human life in terms of oneness. If you practice hard, you can see oneness, you can attain enlightenment, you can experience a lot. But when you return to human existence, see that experience in terms of human eyes and try to repeat it, you never do, because the human world is constantly changing. So all you have to do is, again and again, be in oneness and see the human world from that point of view. How? That is our practice. Do this and then you are called a person who is master of yourself in whatever situation you may be.

22 CHANGING THE STRUCTURE OF TIME AND SPACE

Dogen Zenji mentions that one moment consists of sixty-five instants, or moments. We don't know exactly what the sixty-five moments are, but something is really there, enough to make our life flexible. Within a moment something happens—miracle. That miracle comes from time and space: the unknown sixty-five moments within a moment and the unknown spatial dimension. You don't know time and space exactly, but you can manifest this miracle within the moment you know and the space you occupy.

For instance, if you become a basketball player, you need the power of your individual effort and your group's effort, and you have to master technique. But that is not enough to guarantee that you will win. When you play on a certain day, at a certain time and place, you don't know whether you will win or lose. Even though you have practiced hard, the moment when you start to play, everything becomes zero. So basketball players don't know what will happen, but they hope. What do they hope for? I think they hope for a change in the structure of time and space.

You can change the structure of time and space. How? You have to manifest time and space that you don't know within time and space that you do know. This is not only Zen practice—this is practice for everyone. Whatever you do, your body and mind must be flexible. Usually we attach to our own territory of five *skandhas,* six senses, customs, habits, and memories. We trust the moment we see through our six senses, and we don't trust the unknown sixty-five moments within one moment. But are you sure of your existence, stably and steadfastly? I don't think so. Your own territory is very shaky. To be sure of your existence with confidence, you have to see yourself doing something in the universe with all myriad beings, not in your individual territory. This is difficult, but you have to do it. You have to realize that point in a practical way.

Some people don't believe it is possible to be free from our individual territory, so they say this teaching is abstract. But it really is possible to make this hope become real. How? First, you have to jump into the expanse of the conscious world with full devotion. When you act with full devotion, your physical territory disappears. It is not destroyed—it disappears. But the territory of your consciousness is still left, so how can you be free from your consciousness? That is your practice—activity itself. If you continue to act with full devotion, your consciousness becomes one with your activity, and the form of your consciousness disappears. Your perception of your mind is dissipated, absorbed into the pure sense of simply action itself. When your body and mind are dissipated in full activity, you completely forget yourself.

So basketball players master their individual power, their group power, and their technique, and then they hope. Where do they manifest their hope? In the moment. If you devote yourself to playing basketball with wholeheartedness, the frame of your five *skandhas* and the form of your six senses all disappear within the total manifestation of activity. When only action is there, something happens. You don't know what it is, but something happens.

Athletes don't destroy their body and mind; they just manifest unknown time and space within their body and mind. Then each moment becomes very clear—there is no body and mind there. Then people say, "Beautiful!" If you see the performance of gymnastic athletes on the high bar, it is very beautiful because they become completely zero. By their full devotion to athletic performance, they change the structure of time and space. That's why athletic performance is very beautiful. That's why, if you watch the performance of basketball players, you feel beautiful.

How do we jump into the unknown sixty-five moments within one moment? It's impossible. But what we *can* do is jump into the one moment we know. How can you manifest the sixty-five moments that you don't know within the one moment that you can know? This is the question. It is the question and also your effort, your practice. The structure of a particular time and space is very helpful to you because you can create elasticity there. It is a flexible situation, an opportunity given to you where you can fully devote yourself to doing something and forget yourself. This is how to bloom your flower. At that time you can change the whole situation. You don't know why. It's mysterious, miraculous.

But then people say, "Let's get that miracle!" and it makes people crazy. We grope for something, something that makes us feel good and satisfied, putting knowledge into our heads, emphasizing miracles, technique, and power. But we don't pay attention to the basic activity that is the source of those things. We can experience miracles, but a miracle is just part of impermanence. Sometimes a miracle is good, but sometimes a miracle is not so good. Zen Buddhism doesn't emphasize miracles. We don't pay attention to them. We just come back to the unknown time and space of this very moment, the source of miracles, in every moment of every day. Then, from a miracle, comes a very stable way of life.

23 COMMENTARY ON AN EXCERPT FROM DOGEN'S "ZAZENSHIN"

In *Shobogenzo*, "Zazenshin" (Lancet of Seated Meditation), Dogen Zenji comments on the sayings of Chinese Zen master Nan-yüeh, who is discussing with Master Ma-tsu the nature of zazen and whether one can become a buddha by sitting in meditation:

> If you study zazen, Zen is not sitting and sleeping.
> If you study sitting Buddha, the Buddha is no
> solid form.
> If you become a sitting Buddha, it is a killing Buddha.
> If you attach to the zazen posture, you cannot reach
> to the truth.

When we study Dogen's commentary on these lines, there are three important points to keep in mind. First, what is form? In Buddhism we say there are three stages of understanding reality: form is form, form is not form, and form is form. The first stage is seeing things in the usual objective way, thinking that everything is separate and independent. The second is observing impermanence, realizing emptiness, and deeply understanding that everything is interconnected and nothing has its own solid form. The third is actualizing emptiness in oneness with the forms of daily life.

The second point: how do you live as a human being? Many people who are religious understand the first point very naturally and believe that we are one with the universe, nature, or God. They have a beautiful ideal and try to follow a spiritual life. But the problem is that they don't know how to live according to that ideal in a practical way. How can a human being become one with the universe? What is it that we have to practice? Dogen says we must study and penetrate the present moment. All you can do is approach to this very moment. Simultaneously, you get feedback to support your activities and you know how to behave properly.

Third, what is this very moment? Even though it is difficult to understand, this is important. Otherwise you cannot practice properly. We have to understand very deeply that this very moment is time. Exactly where is time? If you think time is within you, time becomes objective. And if you think time is outside of you, time is also objective. But both are wrong. Time has no solid form—time is activity itself.

BOUNDLESS ACTIVITY

Dogen Zenji introduces the first statement by Nan-yüeh: "Zazen is spoken of as follows: 'If you study zazen, Zen is not sitting and sleeping.'" Then Dogen comments:

> It means that zazen is zazen, not sitting and sleeping. Since the time that not sitting and sleeping is simply transmitted, boundlessness of sitting and sleeping is the self. What is this that you intend to trace the degree of intimacy? How is it that you can

dispute on delusion and enlightenment? Who is in pursuit of wisdom in order to remove delusions?

In Nan-yüeh's statement, "sitting and sleeping" refers to the four kinds of ordinary human activity: walking, standing, sitting, and sleeping, so he is saying that real zazen is not the ordinary activity called sitting. Well, when you do zazen, sometimes zazen is exactly the same as ordinary activity. But sometimes the functioning of the universe appears as zazen. Then zazen is real zazen. For zazen to become real zazen, the form of zazen must be liberated. At that time you say: zazen is zazen.

Saying "not sitting and not sleeping" doesn't deny sitting and sleeping. It means you cannot sit or sleep just in your own territory—you have to sit with myriad, myriad beings. At that time, sitting is nothing but the pure sense of the functioning of the universe, the cosmos. The functioning of the universe appears and zazen becomes a beautiful clear mirror in which the whole universe is reflected. That zazen is completely liberated from ordinary activity.

We can see the functioning of the whole universe in all of our activities—walking, standing, sitting, and sleeping—not just in zazen. When you act wholeheartedly, your activity becomes very clear, calm, flexible, and magnanimous. It is boundless, and simultaneously it is you. So studying the boundlessness of activity is studying the self. This is called intimacy.

How can you know the meaning of intimacy? You cannot see it objectively because intimacy is not the result of activity; intimacy blooms right in the midst of activity itself. If you try to understand intimacy intellectually, as a concept, you never know real intimacy. Delusion and enlightenment are also concepts, but the perfect, supreme state of enlightenment is completely beyond concepts. You are already enlightened, but you can never conceptually know what enlightenment is because when you think of it you create a gap between yourself and enlightenment.

For example, when you swim, if your consciousness picks up one perception of water and a separate perception of swimmer, this is not real intimacy. To experience intimacy with the ocean, you have to jump into the ocean and just swim in the whole universe with no thought of subject and object. Without plunging into the ocean, you can't swim. So open your heart and be intimate with the water. Completely depend on the help of nature. Then the water takes care of you. Your body is supported, your body is swimming, and you survive. You and the ocean are one, and you swim right in the middle of the functioning of the universe. That is great enlightenment.

Plunging into the ocean is your effort. The usual idea of effort implies the egoistic aspect of life. But you should understand swimming from two aspects: something created by your effort and something created by nature's effort. When you make your effort and jump in, you can see the other aspect because something appears that is beyond your effort. The universe is helping you; nature is taking care of your human life. Then swimming is called vivid activity. This swimming is called play—playing with the water, with all sentient beings in the water, and with the five *skandhas* of your body and mind, before you're conscious of them. Your consciousness cannot pin down what intimacy is because consciousness is very picky, always picking out one thing and looking at it separately. So consciousness never knows the true sense of action. But we can know in other ways. You can intuitively know something simultaneously with action. That is our practice.

We are already enlightened beings who are embraced by Buddha's wisdom, because nothing exists outside the ocean of Buddha's world. So all we have to do is deal with life in terms of Buddha's wisdom. But we don't want to do it. We always do the opposite. We always see ourselves in terms of our own viewpoint. No matter how long buddhas and ancestors try to tell us that we are Buddha, we don't feel intimate with Buddha. So let's stop the habit of seeing life just in terms of human perception. Let's see human activity in terms of Buddha's wisdom! Intimacy is not something to discuss—intimacy is activity itself. This is not philosophy—it is something you have to do.

The result of activity is not the important point; the important point is activity itself. Within activity there is a most important motivation called total *samadhi,* or nirvana, so you can deal with every activity in terms of oneness. What does this mean? Your body and your mind must be flexible. When you're flexible, you are totally absorbed into your activity, and that is called *samadhi.* If you try to absorb yourself as your subject into activity as your object, it is not total absorption. In the beginning you have to try, but you cannot do it halfway. To be completely absorbed you have to devote yourself totally, with sincerity, and then you can be absorbed—you can see the unity of your body, your mind, and your object.

In this unity, you give energy to your activity as object, and simultaneously you accept lots of information from your object. That is called total functioning—cause and effect are one simultaneous action of input and output. You give and receive information simultaneously. This is communion of heart with heart, going constantly, in and out. At that time your activity becomes Buddha's activity: time becomes supreme time, beyond any concept of past, present, or future; place becomes supreme place, beyond any dualistic concept; and person becomes supreme person, who is melted into the universe.

That situation is unknowable with our consciousness. It's impossible for me to express it in words. But maybe you can feel that this is true, that Buddha's activity is something that could appear in your life in the future. If so, that feeling becomes a kind of prediction, foreknowledge, or hope. That is called big hope.

What is this hope? Is it to make your life happy? No, this hope is completely beyond your happiness or unhappiness. Of course if you become happy, you feel happy, but it doesn't last for long. In the next moment happiness turns into unhappiness. So what is real hope? We hope to manifest something that we don't know, within the form of bowing in *gassho,* within the form of offering incense, within the form of sitting meditation. This is our hope. Don't you think so? It is possible to make that foreknowledge become real. Hope comes up, you do something with full devotion, you forget yourself, and you change the structure of time and space. Then, even though you don't see it, people feel that.

This practice is not just a teaching for people studying Buddhism—it's for everyone. Any area of the human world—art, music, sports, or whatever you do—requires this way of life. But the question is: What degree of confidence do you have? When you have a very strong, stable confidence every day, it is called spiritual life. If you don't, it is called art, music, or sports. In the practice of art, oneness appears, but outside of art it doesn't work, so you are confused. While playing sports you can understand oneness, but outside of sports you cannot see it because you don't have confidence. When you don't have confidence, the oneness you experience is relative truth. When confidence is always with you, oneness becomes absolute truth. To have strong, stable confidence every day, you must concentrate yourself on making the effort to constantly approach and penetrate this very moment.

APPROACHING THIS VERY MOMENT

Nan-yüeh says, "If you study sitting Buddha, the Buddha is no solid form." And Dogen Zenji's comment is:

> The attempt to speak of sitting Buddha reaches to *immo*. The sitting Buddha manifested by one or two persons is adorned with no solid form. The Buddha's no solid form I speak of is to mention the Buddha's form. Because of Buddha of no solid form, you cannot avoid sitting Buddha. Therefore,

since sitting Buddha is adorned with the Buddha's no solid form, if you study zazen, it is sitting Buddha. Who can take or leave that in terms of dharma of no staying, sitting Buddha is not Buddha or it is Buddha. Since a sense of adoption or rejection drops off from the beginning, it is sitting Buddha.

Wherever you may be, whatever you do, you must approach to this very moment. This very moment doesn't have a form. It's not inside or outside you. This very moment is activity itself, the total dynamic working of the universe, just going constantly. It is "no solid form." That doesn't mean this very moment *has* no solid form; it means this very moment *is* no form at all. When you are approaching to this very moment, you cannot see time objectively, not even slightly, because your activity is time itself. There is no gap where you can think about this moment objectively. But you cannot ignore it, because you are there. So all you have to do is just be present—right here, right now!

Being on an airplane is a good example of being present. If you think about it, taking an airplane is scary. Most people are scared. I think everyone is scared. So why don't people stop taking airplanes? Because they experience something more than being scared—comfort and pleasure too. When you take an airplane, even though there's a chance you could die, all you have to do is just be there. But when I tell you to just be there, you immediately think of yourself objectively and grope for the idea of I. Then "I" splits into two: one I wants to be there, the other I is scared and doesn't want to be there.

But, beyond thinking "I want" or "I don't want" there is total I—the real I. Who is that? How can you manifest total I? You can forget yourself, forget the airplane, and just be present in this very moment. At that time your fear drops off and you can read a magazine in peace.

The same is true of zazen. People usually think that by doing zazen they can get something. They don't understand that zazen is just to act. When you act, within the activity of your zazen all things come together and become one. It's just like the colors on a toy top. When you spin the top, all the colors become one. To practice zazen, all you have to do is just constantly approach to this very moment—just spin. This is the simultaneous activity of subject, object, and all things.

When you do zazen like this, your emotions and delusions drop off. It doesn't mean that you don't have any emotions. No, you cannot be cold dead trees. It means that your emotions work pretty well. You do not destroy or escape from your emotions, but when you practice approaching to this very moment every day, your emotions and delusions naturally drop off by themselves and you are present there, very conspicuously, blooming the flower of your life force. Simultaneously you forget yourself and you are not there. This is called activity—practice in action.

When you are exactly present in this very moment and manifest yourself in total activity, it is called "to observe impermanence." Dogen Zenji mentions very often that if you want to awaken *bodhi*-mind, you have to observe impermanence. It doesn't mean to see impermanence objectively; it means to participate in impermanence itself.

In Buddhism we don't ignore subject or object, concepts or ideas; we try to understand them very deeply through action. Then impermanence as an object and you as a subject are illuminated simultaneously.

Religion usually requires you to believe first and then act. But in Buddhism, to act is simultaneously to believe. So, day by day your zazen must be refined again and again. Pass through the first stage, the second stage, and reach the third stage: zazen is zazen. At the third stage, zazen is called sitting Buddha. This is the pure sense of activity. You are a flower, blooming in the whole universe, and you understand very deeply the meaning of practice related with enlightenment, or truth. This is real zazen. At that time, zazen becomes Buddha. This is called *immo*. *Immo* usually means "what" or "how," but Dogen uses it to indicate truth itself, being as it really is. Sitting Buddha is wonderful! But even though you want to stay with that wonderful moment, you cannot stay. You cannot stay because the universe is constantly changing, and that moment has already gone. So you have to go through the three stages constantly. This is Buddha's expedient method.

Nan-yüeh said, "Buddha is no solid form," but Dogen says that "no solid form" is Buddha. When we see only the pure sense of what we are doing, no solid form is tentatively called Buddha. But if there is no solid form, then who am I? Don't I have a particular solid form called Katagiri? That is just our ordinary understanding. We exist beyond that ordinary understanding.

Your basic nature is no solid form. When you dig the rich ground of your life, many capabilities come up and you're very surprised. If you know yourself very deeply, a wonderful personality comes up, like water in a spring. When no solid form appears in your *gassho,* sitting, walking, or eating, you manifest the form of *gassho* and also something more—emptiness. At that time you cannot avoid Buddha and you manifest zazen or *gassho* as it really is.

If one person manifests the whole universe, one person saves all sentient beings. This seems to be an abstract idea. When you think of it, it becomes abstract because you can't believe it. But it's really true. For example, when Tsugen Narasaki Roshi came from Japan and led a retreat at Hokyoji in Minnesota, he gave a statement. Even though people didn't understand his Japanese, they could see something there. There was something in his *gassho,* in his eyes, or in his standing posture, something that changed the structure of time and space. How could Narasaki Roshi change the spatial structure? It's not a special technique or power. It depends on his intention, how he devotes himself to approaching this very moment. He practices continuously, with no gap. Whatever he does, he manifests dharma, and then the whole situation around him is changed.

Ten people saw Narasaki Roshi give his statement in Minnesota, and ten people were completely drawn into the whole universe through his statement. So we say that ten people were saved. But I don't think there were just ten people there; all sentient beings were there, so all sentient beings were saved. You may say, "I don't understand how all sentient beings can be saved," but I think that someday scientists will know. Maybe they will give you proof.

If you believe that saving all sentient beings is a ridiculous idea, your life is already rigid. Then no matter how long you practice, there is no space to be flexible, no space to manifest the unknown world through the form of your zazen or the form of your standing posture. So try to think why manifesting the unknown world is not an abstract idea, because it's something we have to do right now. We have to manifest the unknown world simultaneously with the known world. This is the point we have to transmit to the next person, to the next generation, whatever age comes.

MANIFESTING CREATIVITY

Nan-yüeh says, "If you become a sitting Buddha it is a killing Buddha." And Dogen Zenji's comment is:

> Eventually, if you study and penetrate further sitting Buddha, the virtue of the killing Buddha can be discovered. The very moment of the sitting Buddha is the killing Buddha. Investigating the distinctive body marks or light of killing Buddha, you never fail to become a sitting Buddha. The term "kill" here, similar though it may be, is quite different from the ordinary people's usage. Killing Buddha in sitting Buddha must be studied and penetrated on what kind of form it lies in. Taking up the truth that there is killing Buddha within the virtue of the Buddha, you should intimately study on killing person and not killing person.

Zen masters in China talked about killing Buddha very often—it's one of their favorite terms—but it doesn't mean to really kill something. It means total actualization and manifestation with no gap, no space to let something extra get in.

If you completely jump into an athletic game, you are melted into the game. If you sit zazen, you are melted into zazen. When no solid form of a person, time, and space all come together and work together, you create a beautiful form. At that time you forget yourself and create your own life. That is called creativity. You can show creativity, but you don't know what it is, so provisionally we say it's a miracle. But it's not really a miracle—it's something alive. When you manifest creativity from moment to moment, it is called killing Buddha. This is wonderful, but Dogen says we have to go beyond this, because the virtue of the killing Buddha can be discovered.

Buddha is something alive, constantly moving. Digest sitting Buddha and it becomes energy for your life. That is called faith, or confidence. This energy is not a philosophical teaching—it's within you already. How can you be one with it in your life? All you can do is constantly, steadfastly, approach to this very moment. Don't attach to an idea of yourself as either form or not-form, because both are impermanent: each appears but in the next moment it disappears. If you attach to one when it appears, you create a discrepancy between yourself and the rhythm of nature. Then when it disappears, you are confused. So just be host to time and place, and then jump in. At that time you can open your heart and meet something with true heart. That experience is called enlightenment, or awakening.

If you manifest creativity in your life, you are manifesting your complete life: form and not-form come together and work together. Where? That is your time and opportunity. When time and opportunity are working within your activity, form and not-form are dissipated, melted right in the middle of total activity. That is called beauty. It is very quiet. Real creativity is manifested in silence. There is nothing to say. All you can do is be present from day to day, from moment to moment.

So, every day, every moment, try to think: Where is the possibility of approaching to this very moment? It's pretty hard, but you have to do it. You must be fresh every single moment. Suffering comes, in the next moment you must be fresh, then suffering dissipates in the dharma world. But then, in the next moment, new suffering comes. So you have to just walk, step-by-step. If you do this, very naturally you become humble and majestic. From generation to generation, buddhas and ancestors have walked like this.

When you really approach this very moment, you show deep kindness. That is called compassion. But if I say, "Be kind!" you immediately imagine the usual sense of kindness and jump into it. Then you are very busy. You have to shake hands with this person, that person, and all the other people. But you cannot shake hands with all of them simultaneously, so something is always missing. Finally you go crazy.

Compassion is not something you try to have. Compassion is when you, your body, your time, and your place all work together. When you manifest creativity in your life, you feel a very deep compassion for your book, your feet, your clothes, and your thoughts. This is called intimacy. You can touch what real kindness is by the way you get dressed in the morning, eat a meal, or sit zazen. You just settle down, right now, right here, and then compassion comes up. If you see a kind, compassionate person like Thich Nhat Hanh, the Vietnamese Zen master, you can see the total functioning of kindness. It's not necessary to explain. You just see him and talk with him.

My teacher always said, "You should take best care of dharma." If I did something a little carelessly, he didn't scold me, he didn't criticize me, he just said, "You should take best care of dharma." I didn't understand what dharma was, but he said it at just the right time, so I felt, "Oh, yes, I made a mistake," and corrected myself. But dharma was a big question for me—a puzzle. So what is dharma? Dharma is truth. But it's not a philosophical idea; we have to find dharma practically. Where? Moment! When time, place, and person are dissipated within this very moment, it is called dharma. At that time we take good care of dharma.

CREATING BEAUTY

Nan-yüeh says, "If you attach to the zazen posture, you cannot reach to the truth." And Dogen Zenji's comment is: "Attaching to the form of zazen means that you have to abandon the usual understanding of the zazen posture and touch the heart of zazen. It is true that you cannot avoid detachment from the zazen posture. Since there is no detaching from the zazen posture, it is not to reach to the truth, even though attaching to the zazen posture is clearly transparent as a jewel."

People usually understand Nan-yüeh's statement to mean: Don't care about form! They think it means that you don't need to be concerned about the form or posture of zazen, because you cannot attain enlightenment that way. But this is a misunderstanding. Dogen Zenji says we have to abandon our usual understanding of the zazen posture and touch the heart of zazen. What is the heart of zazen? To know this, first you have to throw away the usual sense of form. If you touch the heart of the zazen posture, the usual form of zazen is dissipated very naturally.

Touching the heart of form is very important. For example, if you are an expert mountaineer, you have to carry many things when you climb: clothes, boots, food, medicine, ropes, and so on. But if you climb on a hot summer day, the form of the mountain, the form of your body, and the form of your equipment all bother you. You want to climb with your body half-naked, not carrying anything. So why don't you leave all that stuff behind? You cannot do it, because you love being on the mountain. You cannot hate your clothes; you cannot leave your equipment behind. Those things bother you, but you have to carry them. It's not that you *have* to carry them, it's that you *want* to carry them, because without those things you cannot be on the mountain. So it's really love that's bothering you. You love the mountain, so you accept the form of being a mountaineer.

The same applies to the zazen posture or the form of

whatever you do. The zazen posture is really painful, creating lots of stiffness, just like climbing a mountain. But you love something that is at the heart of your life. In order to climb the mountain that is called life, you have to carry a form. It bothers you, but you do it anyway. Then when you touch the heart of form, form creates beauty.

When divers jump from a high cliff into the ocean, they create beautiful athletic art in the air. At that time, the divers are directly connected to the space around them: the cliff, the ocean, their state of mind, and the practice they have done in the past. You cannot see those things because they are completely melted into the form of a dive. Then that form creates a wonderful world. Without the form of the dive, you would not be able to see the beautiful unity of space, cliff, ocean, and diver—you would not be able to see anything at all.

The same is true for the form of zazen. If you practice zazen by throwing away the usual sense of zazen form and touching the heart of zazen form, you see something beautiful. At that time there is nothing to actually see, nothing to actually touch. There are no principles of practice, no training, no discipline, no truth; there is only form. When only form blooms its own flower, there is no space to bring anything into it, not even truth, because it is completely clear and transparent, just like a jewel. This is called creativity.

Within creativity there are two points. One is attachment to form; the other is detachment from form. In detachment, form is still there, but that form is completely different from the usual sense of form. So it means detachment from the usual sense of form. Detachment doesn't mean you should ignore form; it means you have to attach to form through and through. A form may bother you, but you need form because you love truth, you love peace, you love life itself.

When you touch the heart of zazen form and manifest maturity, there is creativity. Within creativity are all the forms you practiced in the past, but creativity itself has no form. You don't know what it is, but like the diver on the cliff, all you have to do is stand up there. All your practice and hard work in the past disappear completely, leaving nothing to depend on. But even though there is nothing to depend on, there is hope. There is a chance to manifest the maturity of all the practice that you have done in the past. How? Jump! Then the whole of existence—past, present, and future—comes together and works together. This is called moment.

Moment is the time and opportunity for you to mature. You cannot wait for oneness to come into you. You have to do something. Act! At that time you become one with nature. This is total manifestation of 100 percent Buddha, creativity in life. Then, within this creativity, your maturity is manifested as a beautiful form.

A diver jumping off the cliff, a mountain climber, an artist, a poet, or a musician creates a beautiful form that manifests the maturity of his or her life. But spiritual life doesn't have that same sense of performance. So creativity in religion cannot manifest in the same way. Of course you do manifest maturity because, as Dogen says, "you cannot avoid detachment from the zazen posture." But then, next you must be free from that manifestation. In

Japanese we say *gedatsu,* meaning emancipation, or freedom. Moment after moment you must be free from the beautiful form you created, because the moment in which that form existed has already gone, and the next moment is coming up. Life becomes mature constantly. You cannot stop it, not even for a moment, so you have to keep going. You must keep practicing to create this beauty again and again. This is spiritual creativity.

So, what is this zazen practice that we do? It's not *doing* zazen. If you believe it's *doing* zazen, then practice is just a task, and that task becomes a really big burden for you. That is not a true understanding of practice. Buddhist practice is to constantly create beauty. Beauty is the functioning of wisdom. That's why Dogen Zenji says that you have to abandon the usual understanding of the form of zazen and touch the heart of zazen. Otherwise you cannot maintain this kind of practice. That's why I have to explain it and why you have to understand very deeply what practice means. Then, if you understand even slightly, you should keep going. That makes your life mature.

24 HOW TO MAKE
YOUR LIFE MATURE

The activity of practice gives you a chance to bloom the flower of your life force and make your life mature. But in order to understand how your life can become mature, first you have to understand the relationship between mind and body. That relationship is just like cloth and design. Mind is a huge cloth, and body is a design on that cloth. The design doesn't exist separately from the cloth, and the cloth doesn't exist separately from the design. In *The Awakening of Faith* there is another analogy: water and waves. Mind is water and body is waves. Waves can't exist separately from water. So water and waves, or cloth and design, work very closely together, intimately. This is the relationship between body as form and mind as consciousness.

According to the Buddhist psychology called Vijnana-vada, consciousness is subdivided into eight consciousnesses: the six sense consciousnesses of sight, sound, smell, taste, touch, and thought; ego-consciousness, called *manas;* and the basic consciousness. The eighth one, basic consciousness, is called *alayavijnana*. This is huge consciousness. We sometimes call this universal life.

Alayavijnana is characterized in several ways. One way is called treasury *vijnana*. Treasury *vijnana* means *alayavijnana* is like a storehouse containing many beings. Myriad, myriad beings from the past to the present to the future are stored there. It is just like a huge ocean. But you cannot see particular things; you cannot separate things. All become one, connected to each other, penetrating each other, and living in peace and harmony.

On the other hand, *alayavijnana* is also characterized as seed *vijnana*. We use the word *seed,* but it doesn't mean a seed like an avocado seed. Seed *vijnana* is a very interesting aspect of basic consciousness. It is going constantly without ever stopping, like the flow of a stream or the flow of a waterfall. If we say that something is going constantly, what is the energy that causes it to survive and go from the past to the present to the future? This is a most important question. To understand your life, you have to understand this point. You have to understand how treasury *vijnana* is connected to the form of your human body by seed *vijnana*.

The Vijnanavada philosophy explains how basic consciousness works. The energy that causes seed *vijnana* to flow is time: the time process and the maturity of time. The maturing of time is the energy that maintains the time process and causes it to go continually. The maturity of time and the time process work together. Mind and body, cloth and design, water and waves, are intimately connected in this way, but this intimacy is very difficult to understand. So let's look more closely at seed *vijnana*.

Traditionally seed *vijnana* is said to work in three steps that function together like a circle. The first step: seed produces seed. Seed constantly produces seed, so seed continues without stopping. This is continuation. The second step: seed produces form. Seed produces its own functioning in the human world of the present. In Japanese we say *gengyo*. *Gen* means "presently" and *gyo* means "functioning, activity, or action." So seed functioning in the present means phenomena. This is form. The third step: form perfumes seed. Seed, which functioned as form in the conscious human world, returns to its source in the unconscious world with a kind of perfume. That perfume makes the seed become mature. Then the energy produced when the seed matures starts the cycle again. This is the time process.

Time is going constantly. Again and again, seed produces seed, seed produces form, the perfume of form matures seed, and seed produces seed again. The functioning of phenomena produces the perfume that makes it possible for time to become mature, and the maturity of time produces the energy that makes it possible for things to change. Time matures in order for life to go one step to the future.

According to this philosophy, the basic consciousness of *alayavijnana* becomes mature in the unconscious world, appears as the form and function of the conscious world, then disappears and returns with a perfume that makes it mature in the unconscious world. Then it appears again as a new world of form and function. If the seed didn't appear on the surface of consciousness as the phenomenal world of body, design, or wave and then become mature in the unconscious world of mind, cloth, or water, life would never have a chance to mature. There would be no energy, no time process, and no change.

Your life is maturing from moment to moment. You

cannot stop it. But you can manifest that maturity through your form. Your form is your everyday life. In order to manifest maturity in your life, you need form, because without form you would never have a chance to make yourself mature. Then the form of your everyday life is an indication of your maturity.

We always pay attention just to the waves on the surface of our lives and try to make our lives mature through the six senses. This is fine, but still you have to pay attention to how the deep level of existence is functioning and maturing your life. In order to make the surface of your life mature, you have to make the depth of your life mature.

The depth of human life is directly connected to the surface of everyday life. Everydayness perfumes the depth of life, the huge ocean where all are interconnected, and makes your life mature. Then a new life arises from the depth and appears on the surface. So, by taking care of everydayness, you don't make just the surface mature; you also make the depth of your life mature. That is the most important point!

You don't know how deep your existence is: sometimes it's an abyss; sometimes it's paradise. But even though you don't know the depth of human life, it's there in your everyday life. That's why I always say, "Let's take care of everyday life!" How? That's why we practice. If you touch something deep, you understand how you can cause your life to mature by the activity of taking care of everyday life.

Taking care of everyday life is not the same as trying to fix everything neatly. Most people are upset and confused by problems and want to escape from suffering. They rush into fixing problems—running here and there to find a good person to fix their life, trying to get a result quickly by psychology or philosophy—but they forget about fixing the depth of life. Fixing problems is part of life, but it's not the main point, it's secondary. The main point is our attitude toward the problem. I don't mean you should ignore fixing or adjusting human life, because it is very important to do that. But if you attach to fixing as your primary way of life, that way of life leaves you in bewilderment, because no matter how long you try to fix everything, you cannot fix everything perfectly. So there is something more important that you have to do.

Within each single problem there is an important opportunity to make the depth of your life mature. To realize this opportunity, first you have to throw away the usual sense of suffering and touch the heart of suffering. Deal with suffering right in the middle of suffering. Then suffering gives you lots of instruction. Whether you have a problem, pain, or pleasant feeling in zazen, please sit. That's it! You must be tranquil and calm down. Otherwise you can't see the panoramic picture of how existence is functioning every day.

Sit in zazen, calm your six sense consciousnesses, and then quiet the egoistic *manas* consciousness. At that time, basic consciousness touches all things, without exception—the whole universe. That is *alayavijnana,* the serene and tranquil state of consciousness that is the original nature of human life. This mind of tranquillity is called *bodhi*-mind, universal consciousness, or the Buddha Way.

Whether you are conscious of it or not, your life exists right in the midst of Buddha's path, called mind, *tao*, or the way. All beings go along this path. It is open not only to human beings but to all beings—animate or inanimate. All sentient beings are walking together hand in hand on Buddha's path.

The universal path is complete tranquillity and at the same time constantly flowing. It exists forever, constantly supporting all beings. But to make it something that is alive in your life, you have to do something; you have to touch it directly with full awareness and turn it into reality. Through practice you become one with *alayavijnana* and experience the stillness of the original nature of existence. Then time matures, *alayavijnana* works dynamically, and the human form called buddha or bodhisattva appears in the phenomenal world.

When I talk about Zen practice I always say, "Just do it!" because action makes action. If you act, something is left behind that drives you to do more, because seeds constantly produce seeds in the bottom of human consciousness. That is the characteristic of *alayavijnana* that is just like a waterfall, going constantly. There's a kind of momentum.

Action itself is momentum. You cannot separate the two, because action puts you right in the middle of momentum. When you are right in the middle of that momentum, you can see many things coming up from the depth of existence. From moment to moment all things in the phenomenal world come up—the whole universe comes up. That is practice in action.

If you practice and penetrate this very moment, you

are absorbed into the flow of that undefiled, clear, and pure activity. Then when you do something, you feel something wonderful. You cannot explain it, but this is creativity in life. It's beautiful! Everything is there, melted into your form and clear like a jewel. If you become a sportsman or artist, you can do this in a certain area of life. But in spiritual life, it must be done in *every* area of life. You have to create this every day, in every daily routine. That's pretty hard. But through this form of practice your life becomes mature and you can live your life smoothly in peace and harmony.

If you want to learn the total picture of human life, you have to tune in to the rhythm of life, the melody of the universe. Doing this is called spiritual life. It is arousing the thought of enlightenment. Arousing the thought of enlightenment is arousing *bodhi*-mind, the way-seeking mind, as motive for religious or spiritual action. Then, by virtue of activity based on the way-seeking mind, you can see deeply into the structure of the phenomenal world of everyday life called the samsaric world. You see the truth of how human life is going, and you experience wisdom.

If you think about wisdom objectively, it is called the principle of existence, the principle of the universe, or truth. But if you see truth clearly and actually touch it, you digest that principle in your heart and the principle is transformed from an idea into something that is present in your life. Something wonderful fills your heart, and the principle of existence is transformed into wisdom. That is the experience called enlightenment, or *bodhi*. Then, based on the peace and harmony of wisdom, you build up everyday life. That is your final goal, which is called nirvana.

Nirvana is the generous, magnanimous state of existence where all aspects of human experience come in and are digested, moment after moment, creating complete peace. Nirvana is not enlightenment; it is everyday life based on wisdom. Standing in the realm of wisdom and seeing the truth, you think deeply: How can I build up everyday life? This is our aspiration or hope. That is called arousing *bodhi*-mind.

Arousing *bodhi*-mind means taking a vow to save all sentient beings before thinking of one's self. Spiritual practice is dynamic human action based on that motive. To accomplish your aspiration or hope, you devote yourself, giving your body and mind under all circumstances. When you really devote yourself to doing something, you go beyond the time process and forget time. That's why your life is very stable there. This is the characteristic of *bodhi*-mind that is called going beyond time and space.

Arousing *bodhi*-mind is not imagining something divine that is somewhere far away from you in heaven. Thinking in that way is delusion. Real *bodhi*-mind is alive in your everyday life. That's why you can enter real practice. Practice leads you to forget your self-consciousness. When there is no self-consciousness, it is called enlightenment. Your consciousness becomes one with your activity, you forget time, and you experience wisdom. Then something peaceful comes forth in your everyday life and is manifested in the samsaric world. Something appears that changes the structure of time and space. That is called nirvana. Then you really want to do something for all sentient beings, so you arouse *bodhi*-mind again.

The four activities: arousing *bodhi*-mind, practice, enlightenment, and nirvana have not the slightest break.

They go continually in the orbit of a circle that is beginningless and endless. That's why, in the great way of the buddhas and ancestors, there is always continuous practice. Continuous practice is the way without beginning or end. It means to go without stopping at all, not even for a moment. It is very refined action, the pure and clear nature of human action.

If you seek the spiritual life, every action must be like this. Zazen must be based on these four activities' going on without stopping even for a moment. This simple practice, called *shikantaza,* or just sitting, has been handed down from generation to generation; it is for everyone, universal. It is continuous practice that goes on forever, not for the sake of accomplishing your individual purpose or goal, but for all sentient beings.

Whatever sport, art, or profession we follow, we always go in the direction of using our individual talent and capability to accomplish our individual purpose, with the goal of satisfying our individual desire. This is the usual way of life. But people who seek a spiritual way of life always go in the direction of wanting to save all sentient beings, not just satisfy individual desire. So a buddha's or bodhisattva's way of life is completely different from the usual way. It's different from sports or the arts, because there's no accomplishment to show others what you have done. Even if you get a result, you have to let it go. You have to completely offer your body, your mind, and your whole life to the universe. That's pretty hard.

Usually we have a purpose for giving: we want to give something to somebody who will give us something in return. Or we do something for the sake of success in our careers or for the development of our personalities. But spiritual life is not done for a particular purpose—it's huge. Zen practice is just to open the heart and be intimate with the truth. It's very vague. You don't understand it. But finally, if we do something successfully, we have to give it back to all sentient beings. That is the bodhisattva's vow.

When you vow to do something for others, even if it's just a small detail, you really give your whole body and mind to doing it. This is your practice. Then, based on right seeing of truth and right thinking of what to do, you can walk the spiritual path of right activity in everyday life. Zen practice is based on the continuous merging of wisdom and compassion. One by one, each of us should practice in that way. A religious person must be a good friend who can walk hand in hand, side by side with people, whoever they are, without losing the spiritual way of life. To do this, first of all we should awaken ourselves to where we are and what we are doing. This is wisdom. Then we should help others.

The bodhisattva vow to save all sentient beings isn't based on an evaluation. It's not thinking that all sentient beings need to be saved based on ideas of good or bad, right or wrong. A bodhisattva vows to save all sentient beings because most people don't know where they are. We are already in the ocean of Buddha's world, but we don't know where the water is. We are confused. We are already great beings, but we don't realize it, so we create problems.

For example, I use reading glasses. Some people hang their glasses around their necks, but I don't. After I use my glasses, I put them down someplace. The other day I wanted to read the dictionary, but I couldn't find my glasses. I was looking all around for them. Finally I realized the glasses were on top of my head. It's ridiculous! This is what is called confusion. We are already in Buddha's world, but we don't realize it. That's why a bodhisattva has to be compassionate and try to show all sentient beings where the water is, tell them they are already in the water.

When you help others, don't bring an evaluation based on good or bad, right or wrong. Just help all sentient beings, wherever they are. All sentient beings are already Buddha. To awaken them is just to remind them of the truth. Just open your heart and be intimate with the truth. When you realize where the glasses are, just say, "Here they are!" with no sense of evaluation. That's enough.

Spiritual practice has a great power to help all sentient beings. If you practice, you can have great influence. When you stand or when you do zazen, it's beautiful, and people are very moved by your posture because the power and influence of truth is there. But spiritual power is not something you create on the surface of your life. Real spiritual power is the power behind power. The power behind power is the true meaning of effort. It is pure action without needing a particular goal. Instead of expecting to get a result from our effort, we give quality to our effort. This is a very important practice for us. That's why spiritual life is very calm, very quiet, and very stable. That's why *you* can be very stable and calm.

The same applies to sports, painting, dancing, music, or any kind of art. Real beauty is behind the beauty you can see or hear. For instance, look at a beautiful painting. You cannot say why you feel beautiful when you see it, but you know there is beauty there. People ask you why it is beautiful and you can't explain, but you can feel it. Why do you feel beautiful when you see the ballet? There is the great power of ballet behind the ballet dancers' individual power. When you see them, their beauty touches your heart and helps you.

Spiritual life is vast, and you cannot get a result immediately, but you can practice it continually, with full devotion, in every aspect of your life. When you practice in the *zendo,* you can concentrate your body and mind on the form of zazen or *gassho.* When you are walking on the street or sitting in your office, there is no particular form for you to concentrate on, but you can concentrate on breathing. Breathing is very close to you, and also it's alive. To breath is to live. That's why we concentrate on breathing.

By your full devotion, the phenomenal world and unknown time and space come together and work together in your life—right here, right now. At that time you are calmly, stably walking on Buddha's path, and you live freely in peace and harmony. The beauty of existence appears in your life as the functioning of wisdom, and your action is right because it is manifesting the truth. The human form called buddha or bodhisattva arises as time and space, and that form really helps people. So let's walk together with hope and make our life mature. Then, by compassionate action based on wisdom, we can help all sentient beings move one step toward the future. That's pretty good for us.

The theory of karma is one of Buddha's teachings on how to understand human life and how life is going toward the future. It is a big subject, a very important subject that we have to study in order to know how to live in this world.

The study of karma requires us to carefully examine human life in the long term: past, present, and future. To understand karma we have to understand the dynamic functioning of time in the appearance and disappearance of moments, the emptiness that allows life to change, and the arising of a moment of life according to interconnected and constantly changing causes and conditions. From moment to moment we are born, exist as human beings, die, and return to the vast universe. Next moment there is new life. Karma works within this constant process of birth and death.

Karma according to Buddhism does not have the common meaning that people usually think of. So don't misunderstand karma. Karma is not the idea that your personal future depends on a divine creator, chance, or fate. If you believe that a divine creator produces everything, consciously or unconsciously you think there is some kind of manipulative divine entity who has your life on a string, so you don't know how to deal with your own future. If you believe that everything is produced by accident or fortuity, you cannot do anything with purpose because you think that whatever you do, everything happens by chance anyway. If you believe in fatalism, you think that everything is ordained by a pattern that was set up in the beginningless past, and no one can change it. When you lead your life according to chance or fatalism, there is no reason to make any effort and no beautiful dream for the future. You lose the optimistic spirit of human effort, and you become pessimistic. But when you really look at your life, you cannot say that something controls your life, because your life is yours—you still have to handle your own life every day. You cannot say that everything happens by chance or fate, because you see that, in many ways, you create your life by your own effort.

When you study Buddhism and investigate karma, you don't understand exactly what karma is because karma is very complicated. I don't think it's necessary to get a definite answer to what karma means, but you should try to get a certain hint, a practical feeling about it, through your body and mind, through your everyday life.

Karma is not something pessimistic. If you think of karma as something wrong, you are seeing karma only according to what happened in the past. You look at the past and karma becomes a monster. So you should also look at karma in the present and future. Then karma becomes something very wide and really alive. Through karma you can understand what your destiny is. Destiny itself has no solid form; it's something you can create. You can create your life. That is why we study karma.

27   WHAT IS KARMA?

Karma in Buddhism means to act, to work, or to do. Buddhism doesn't separate mental and physical acts, so "to act" includes both mental and physical action. According to common sense, it seems that human action is not carried forward for long. It seems that if you scream, it's just a scream. Your scream is in the present and will not be carried into the future. But according to the idea of karma, that's not all. After you scream, something is still there. Can you imagine? That is called perfume. Something is left behind, not as a shadow, but as something in your body and mind. This is karma. Where is it? In what part of your life does karma exist? For twenty-five hundred years Buddhists have tried to understand this.

Early Buddhism used the Sanskrit term *yoni,* meaning something stored in the womb. Then, in the *Abhidharmakosa* there are the terms *kalalam,* which is the first seven days of a pregnancy, and *arbudam,* the second seven days. The *Abhidharmakosa* is based on the old Buddhist psychology that examines how you produce your life, including your past, present, and future. In that scripture, karma is something like a continuous energy somewhere in human life. It's a little vague, but maybe in the first or second seven days of life there is a certain energy—a very basic, continuous stream of human energy—that exists prior to your human consciousness.

Mahayana Buddhism developed the psychology called Vijnanavada, which means merely consciousness. According to Vijnanavada, there is unmanifested karma, or unmanifested matter or form, that represents a kind of potential power in human life. Another term in Mahayana Buddhism is *alayavijnana,* the last of the eight consciousnesses after the six sense consciousnesses and ego-consciousness. *Alayavijnana* is basic consciousness, a very deep consciousness beyond the usual idea of conscious or unconscious. It has another name, *karma vipaka,* which means a kind of storehouse of various acts that you have accumulated for a long time. It's a huge storehouse of human acts. That is your individual life, but also there is a certain potential power there that belongs not only to human life but to everything. *Alayavijnana* is universal; people, tables, and trees all have *alayavijnana.*

Buddhist psychology continued to develop in the *Avatamsaka Sutra,* which presents a very clear, definite structure that explains how the human world is going. If you read that sutra, you don't understand it, because it presents a very complicated philosophy and psychology. But in that sutra, karma is understood not only as potential mental or physical power but also as a kind of energy in the stream of existence called interdependent co-origination. The very deep Mahayana philosophy of interdependent co-origination explains that everything is produced by conditioned elements, which are always creating an energetic stream that is completely beyond thought, beyond control. Karma works within interdependent co-origination, so karma belongs not just to a particular being but to the depth of existence in general—cosmic existence.

Karma is vast. It's not something you completely understand through your intellect; karma can only be understood by something more than your intellect. It's something you understand from a dispassionate and imperturbable perspective. If you see, very deeply, the structure of human existence, you can see the actual reality behind the philosophy, how complicated it is. Karma is not fate or destiny. Well, maybe it's a kind of fate or destiny, but karma includes a dynamic energy to make your life productive. Everyone can feel this. So you can use karma even though you don't understand it.

28 THE LAW OF CAUSATION

When we consider our future life and destiny, we have to think about it according to the idea of karma. We can think of karma as a kind of energy that is produced by our actions. There are three kinds of activity: physical deeds of the body, linguistic deeds of the mouth, and mental deeds of the mind. Deeds produce the stream of causation, so there is cause and effect. Karma is based on the laws of causation: good cause produces good result, evil cause produces evil result, and neutral cause produces neutral result. If you did something good in the past, there is a good result in the present, and if you did something wrong in the past, there is an evil result in the present.

The natural and common understanding of cause and effect is that if you do something good, you will get a good result, but causation is not so simple. You might do something good and *not* get a good result. You work hard your whole life, but you are still poor. Or you do something bad, but the result is not bad. If you rob a bank, you might be put in jail for several years, or you might not get caught. You might be free and rich because you stole lots of money. Yet you cannot ignore the characteristic of causation that good cause brings good result and evil cause brings evil result. So we can think of three kinds of retribution: cause will bring result in this life, in the next life, or in the life after the next life. In other words, life is going constantly, life after life.

Another law of causation is: if you do something with a bad motivation, even if you don't get caught, what you did hasn't ended. Something is left behind and you don't feel good. In that case, the result you get is a feeling of guilt. On the other hand, if you do something with a good motivation, you may not get a good result but still you feel good. You feel pleasure. Good and bad feelings are not the same as good or bad results, because feeling good or bad is something very personal, completely beyond the measure of good or bad, right or wrong. So when the result of doing something is a feeling, it is called neutral in nature. Most people are completely tossed away by good and bad feelings because they attach to them and then they suffer. But in terms of causation, a feeling is just something to accept from your past life. Then a feeling doesn't tie up your life—it gives you a chance to deepen yourself.

The karma of what you did in the past exists right now, right here. When you see that karma, maybe you don't feel good, but keep your mouth shut and just feel it! Experience it! Accept feeling good. Accept feeling evil. If you did something wrong in the past, you have to accept the result, but you are still free to do something good now. So carry your feeling, reflect upon yourself, and carefully think about what to do in the next moment. From moment to moment you have a chance to move toward the future. If you do something good now, there will be a good result in the future. Karma should be understood like this.

So first, totally accept your life and what you did in the past. Then, based on the past, make a choice about what to do in the present, and by your decision you can create a new life in the future. That is the real meaning of freedom. Freedom is the vastness of existence where you can accept your past and create your new life moving toward the future. But there is no freedom without limitation. Freedom must be created within limitation. Within the limitation of karma from the past, there is a chance to create a new life. Whatever you did, this is true. So accept responsibility for your life. Then, with your free will, make a choice.

For example, if you want to be a doctor you can choose to go to school. But if you go to school, you have to throw away the freedom to choose and accept the limitations created by being in school. Then limitation doesn't bother you. You can stay in school, continue to study, and create your new life toward the future. But if you don't accept the limitation of school and want to keep free will, it's pretty easy to drop out.

If you are interested in Zen Buddhism, you are free to decide what to do. You can go to a Zen center for practice and study. Then if you don't like that place, that's okay, go someplace else. That is a choice you make with your own free will. But if you choose to stay and practice at a Zen center, there are limitations, rules and regulations. So with your freedom you can make a choice, but after making the choice you should throw away your freedom and practice according to the rules and regulations. Then you can create your destiny, the new life you are interested in, because your deeds are causes and your future life is the result.

In Japan fortune-tellers sit in front of the railroad stations. They tell you about your future by looking at your hands, your face, your body, or maybe by your smell. If a fortune-teller tells you, "Oh, your life is bad!" that's all right. Maybe the fortune-teller sees your destiny, but that is just a part of human life, it is not the overall picture. Don't worry! Just accept it, because your destiny is telling you something: there is something stinky about your life. Just accept that stinkiness as a limitation from your past life. Accept your past life as it is, because without your past life you could not make a choice in your present life. Then stinkiness doesn't bother you; it gives you a useful hint. You can do something now to change your future life. In the next moment, stinkiness disappears. That is the idea of karma.

29   INDIVIDUAL AND
NOT-INDIVIDUAL KARMA

The law of causation seems simple, but actually the stream of causation is not so simple because everything is interconnected. Based on the past, you can make a choice in the present, but you cannot make your choice just by yourself—you have to make your choice with all sentient beings. For instance, I made a choice and now I am a Zen teacher. This is my choice, but my decision doesn't come only from me; it comes both from my decision and also other people's decisions. Without other people choosing to be students, I could not make the choice to be a teacher.

Karma is big and vast. It comes from what you did with your own free will, but you did not create karma by yourself. Karma is something done by you with other people, society, all sentient beings, and all circumstances. So it's very complicated.

There are two kinds of karma: individual and not-individual. Everything has both kinds of karma. Individual karma is individual character. There is a certain character in everything, so a microphone is different from the table you put it on. Not-individual karma is karma that is common, or shared with other beings.

In your own case, you have your individual character

and you are a human being. If you are an American, you have your individual karma and the shared karma called American, which is your culture and society. If you go to Europe, you may look like the people who live there, but the people there see something different about you and say, "Oh, you are American." There is the individual character of a nation, and there is also the character common to human beings. For a human being, having two kinds of karma means that if you do something in any of the three categories of action—body, speech, and thought—you create not only your own life but also the life of your family, community, culture, and all human society.

When you ignore the fact that you belong to a group, society, or nation and only try to develop your individual karma, you may develop your character, but that development is based on ego. For instance, if you live with another person, how do you live together in peace? How do you develop your own personality in that situation? It's not so simple. You think, "I want to live with you, but on the other hand, I want to live my own way." Or you want to marry, but in the next moment you want to divorce. This is egoistic.

In America I am different from most people because I am Japanese. But I have to give Buddha's teaching in a way that is beyond race and culture. I am different, but I am present in the universe. So I can walk together with all people and try to develop my own personality with all beings. When you develop your individual character in the broad perspective of not-individual karma, then your personality develops very gently, in a humble way.

Sometimes Americans who study Zen Buddhism don't want to follow the Japanese way of practice. Instead of following Japanese customs they want an American way of Buddhism. That is really an intellectual understanding. So I always say, "Pat your head and go beyond your intellectual understanding." We have to develop the character of an American way of Buddhism by taking care of human life, because American karma is not separate from human karma. Can we understand America separate from Europe and the East? No, there is no way. If you want an American way of Buddhism to develop naturally, pay attention to the entire cosmic situation. Nevertheless, you have to develop your own character. How? Humbly.

The American spirit is very energetic. That energetic spirit can be developed in a humble way by understanding that whether you are American, Japanese, or European, you are human beings. Even though you are different from others who do not share your culture and society, you are human beings, so in many ways you are the same. It's complicated, but you have to take care of it in a practical way.

We have to be careful how we act and how we develop our lives because a human being is a peaceful being and also something stinky. For example, we created nuclear weapons that may destroy all beings. Were those weapons created by a particular race? No, human beings created them. That is part of the global character of human beings. We can't ignore it. We have to develop as individuals within the character that all human beings possess.

Each of us must take responsibility for what we do personally *and* as a member of human society because when we develop our individual character, we simultaneously develop the global character of human beings. We have to do this beyond ego, beyond any expectation that we can build a peaceful world that way. That's why Thich Nhat Hanh says, "Breathing in I calm my mind and body. Breathing out I smile with joy." So, beyond our intellectual ideas, let's be peace. This is our practice. Day by day we have to build up peace within the complicated existence of human beings. Religiously speaking, this is our peace work.

30 MANIFESTED AND
UNMANIFESTED KARMA

Karma is within individual life, so we have to take responsibility for our actions. But on the other hand, karma is beyond individual control. This is a very contradictory situation: karma is ours and simultaneously not ours. If we want to understand karma and how to be free from karma, we have to study this point.

According to Buddhist psychology, karma is divided into manifested karma and unmanifested karma. Manifested karma is something that appears in a moment and disappears. Human action appears on the surface of life, and the next moment it is gone. Zen teachers sometimes say, "Just be present, here and now!" so you may think this means that when you do something you should just take care of human action that appears on the surface. But that is really a messy way of life. If you pay attention only to what manifests on the surface of life, you don't understand human beings, because there is something else—unmanifested karma.

Unmanifested karma occupies the basis of human existence. Whether you realize it or not, whatever you do, your action leaves behind a kind of smell in the depth of human life. We have to take responsibility for our behavior, whatever it is, good or bad, right or wrong, because even though our actions disappear from the surface of life, the smell of what we have done is still there as unmanifested karma. If you don't understand that there is unmanifested karma, you cannot understand the depth of human life, and you don't realize the importance of your actions.

Everyone carries the unmanifested karma of human action from the beginningless past as a sort of inheritance or property. It's not something like original sin; it's completely nothing. You simply cannot put any label like good or bad, right or wrong on unmanifested karma, because it is completely beyond the moral sense. So I use the term *neutral nature*. This karma is always present in your life, stored in your body and mind. If it doesn't appear on the surface, no one knows it's there. You don't know either, so it doesn't bother you. The fact that unmanifested karma doesn't bother you is its neutral nature.

No one knows how to open the door to that big storehouse of karma at the depth of human life, but there *is* something that can open the door—time and occasion. When time is ripe and conditions are arranged, something happens. The door suddenly opens, bubbles come up to the surface, and human action appears.

I smoked cigarettes for many years. I didn't want to smoke, but my original motivation was to help my father. My father was almost blind. He couldn't see the candle or charcoal to light his cigarettes, so I always helped him. I lit a cigarette and took a puff before I gave it to him. The first puff was pretty good, so I inhaled it. Then I was sick, very often. Every time I got sick, I decided that I would never smoke again. I told my father, "You smoke by yourself!" but I couldn't convince him. Finally, I was a cigarette smoker.

Then I was always thinking, "I should stop this someday." You know that smoking is not good, so you think, "I will stop." But the next moment, you want to start. You stop for two days, a week, or sometimes three months, but you start again. Finally I said, "How stupid I am!" so I stopped. But even though I decided to stop, smoking really interested my body. Someone smokes a cigarette in front of you and says, "Hey, Katagiri, why don't you smoke?" You say, "No, I quit smoking." But, "Come on, one puff." So you smoke.

Something always compels you to smoke again. Your will says, "No, I don't smoke," but something happens and you smoke. Why? There is a very simple reason: time and occasion. Conditions are arranged and you smoke. Those conditions are closely related with the karma of your past actions. When you smoked in the past, you left something, an impression that remained behind. It was stored, piled up in your life, until something happened. Then, when conditions are arranged, it appears and you smoke again.

But there is always hope for freedom from that karma. Using your will you have to try again and again. Whatever you do, under all circumstances, you have to think, "I want to stop smoking." I was always aiming at, hoping for that perfect situation when I could quit smoking. The perfect situation, when time is ripe and conditions are arranged, is beyond your individual control. But if you constantly aim at that big hope, then, when the time is ripe and the conditions are arranged for you to stop, you are there, right on the moment. At that time, very naturally, you stop smoking.

That happened to me at Sokoji Temple in San Francisco during a seven-day *sesshin*. At a *sesshin* there is no smoking. Of course you can smoke outside, but I thought, "Oh, this is a good chance, so let me stop smoking." Then my will, environment, and other people all encouraged me. The time was ripe and the conditions were arranged, so I just stopped smoking. And after that I didn't worry. I didn't think about whether or not I would smoke again. But even though I don't smoke now, there is no guarantee that I quit. Probably I could smoke again, because I still carry my karma. Time and conditions could open that door, because the karma from my past is stored in my life.

Unmanifested karma has a neutral nature. It's not good or evil—it's quiet. If you don't touch it, it doesn't appear. "You don't touch it" means that you don't create the time, occasion, and conditions for it to appear. If conditions aren't arranged, unmanifested karma doesn't appear. When you are always trying to do something good, very naturally you don't create conditions where you want to do something wrong. In this way you store good karma, and bad karma doesn't appear.

Unmanifested karma is stored into the future, so we should do something good, helping people. Then our action leaves an impression on our life that we carry toward the future. If you create good karma every day, you store good karma in your life, but it can't appear unless time and conditions are arranged. They may be arranged naturally or arranged by you, but when time and conditions are arranged, karma appears.

Karma is really the source of individual life, within us and simultaneously not ours. Through spiritual practice you can deeply understand the presence of karma in human life. You see that you exist right in the middle of a huge world that is appearing and disappearing from moment to moment, and you realize that your life is interconnected with all beings. Then you want to take good care of your interconnected life, and you begin to think deeply on how to use your consciousness, your will, and your determination to create good karma and to create opportunities for good karma to appear in the human world.

31   KARMA AND CAUSATION

Broadly speaking, if you say "karma" it means both individual karma that is yours and universal karma that is completely beyond human control. All human beings are exactly the same: analyzing, synthesizing, and trying to understand the truth intellectually. We are all deluded because we have human consciousness, so we don't know exactly what the truth is. That is the universal karmic nature of the human world, called dualism. But in the dualistic world, there are many different types of human life.

Why were you born in this world? Why are you different from other people? Why do you act in a particular way? Strictly speaking, you don't know exactly why. But there is some reason, because you are here. That is your individual karma. This karma is what you have done from the beginningless past, connected to your heredity, personality, education, customs and habits, and so on. How does your karma last from the beginningless past up to your present life? This is a big question.

Everything in the dualistic world exists according to the law of causation. For something to exist, first there must be a cause of its existence. But the theory of causation also includes the conditions that surround a cause and effect. Conditions are not the same as causes. For example, seed and pumpkin: seed is cause and pumpkin is effect. The seed is the cause of the pumpkin's existence, but the seed can't grow into a pumpkin by itself. It needs conditions: sunshine, warmth, humidity, soil, water, human effort—many things. These are called secondary causes, or conditioned elements.

According to Buddhist teaching, everything in the phenomenal world is produced by the interrelationship of cause and effect and myriad conditioned elements. Cause and effect implies seeing the world in terms of the time process: past, present, and future. On the other hand, conditioned elements exist not only in the dimension of time but also in the dimension of space. We see the total picture of one thing in terms of time and space working together, so we say everything is produced by causes and conditions.

One thing that exists right now, right here, is like a huge pyramid. At the top of the pyramid there is one existence, so-called Katagiri, but around Katagiri's existence there is a huge world of conditioned elements that interconnect with the past, present, and future. There are countless numbers of conditions around one cause and effect. So there are many reasons why something is produced. That's why you see different types of human life.

In Buddhism existence is interdependent co-origination. The philosophy of interdependent co-origination explains how the phenomenal world arises from the source of existence at the intersection of time and space—right now, right here—produced by the functioning of twelve interconnected links of causes and conditions. These twelve links take life from the past to the future.

The first two links are called ignorance and formative forces. These links represent the world of the past as cause and condition for the present. Ignorance is not something you create in the present; it comes from the universe before you are born. Ignorance is the incipient moment, the origin of energy. Then, immediately, you really want to be. That is the origin of human will, or volition. When the energy of ignorance is exercised as human will, it becomes formative forces. The functioning of formative forces is the energy that puts everything together. Put together, everything is interconnected. That is the world of the past.

Then, in the world of the present, you accept five results coming from past causes: human consciousness; name and form; six sense organs; tangibility, or contact; and perception, or feeling. Human consciousness is characterized by dichotomizing, discriminating, analyzing, and synthesizing. Without your dualistic human consciousness you cannot exist, but this consciousness creates a gap. The first moment you are in your mother's womb, you try to catch something, make a choice, and get a chance.

After you are in your mother's womb, there are names for brain, nerve, eye, nose, and so on, and those forms are created. The six sense organs produce the senses of seeing, hearing, smell, taste, touch, and thought. Then you are born and contact objects in the human world. That is tangibility, the indication of your existence. When you come in contact with the human world, you can learn something by perception. These are the five results coming from ignorance and formative forces in your past life that you have to accept in your present life. Then, in the present, you produce three causes and conditions that will be carried toward the future: attachment (craving), grasping (clinging), and being. In the future there are two more: life, and finally, old age and death.

Karma has a deep meaning based on the theory of interdependent co-origination. In the twelvefold chain of conditioned causation, karma is formative forces, which is the second link, called *samskara* in Sanskrit. Karma is also being, which is the tenth link, called *bhava*. *Samskara* is the first stage of human movement, and *bhava* is your existence in the human world. The quality of karma as *samskara* is ignorance, the first link, which is called *avidya*. *Avidya* is not karma, but it is a quality of karma, because ignorance is the origin of the energy that causes *samskara* to exist.

In *The Awakening of Faith* it says that the meaning of ignorance is that the mind moves. The mind moving is a very minute vibration that is difficult for us to recognize. That is the incipient moment. The very minute movement of mind is called moment. Moment is not time you can see objectively; moment is with you exactly. In a moment, mind moves and life begins, based on ignorance, before we are conscious of it. For this reason we speak of ignorance as beginningless. It means that ignorance comes from the beginningless past as a very minute vibration of consciousness.

The first stage of the vibration of consciousness is the first stage of ignorance. This ignorance is the basic nature of human life. We say that ignorance is rooted in the bottom of human existence because our dualistic human consciousness is based in that first stage of ignorance. If you try to know it, it's very evasive, because it's connected with the vastness of existence. We don't know where this ignorance comes from, but whether you are conscious of it or not, it is there. If you want to understand, you have to examine yourself very deeply—through zazen, through everyday life—then you can touch the bottom of your human life and see what exists there: just ignorance, a very minute mind movement, constantly going. Then, through the realization of ignorance, you can see the vastness of existence, which is called emptiness, or truth. That's pretty good for us.

How does the mind move? That is by the coming together of many causes and conditions. When time is ripe and conditions are arranged, mind moves and ignorance comes up. Mind itself is constantly moving. *The Awakening of Faith* explains it as the relationship between water, wind, and wave. Water is mind itself, which is deep and calm. Wind is the conditions around human life. There are many countless conditions around the surface of water, and because of them water starts to move. That is wave. Waves are the myriad aspects of human life. Waves constantly come up from water according to conditions and seem to have their own existence. So right after mind moves you see waves. But wind and waves are nothing but conditions that arise from mind, completely beyond your human speculation. That is called ignorance. When you see waves, sometimes you like them and then you really want to be there, or sometimes you hate waves and then you try to keep away from them. That is attachment and grasping.

In the chain of conditioned causation, the three links of ignorance, attachment, and grasping are called delusions. By these delusions we create karma, and by karma we create suffering. The suffering you create now is your human mind and body. In the future you will have life, and old age and death, which are also suffering. Strictly speaking, the cause of human suffering is not ignorance; it's attachment. Attachment is called direct cause. Ignorance is just the mind movement. Attachment is the concrete aspect of ignorance, so you can see it through your everyday life.

Delusions are causes of suffering because, according to the karma of formative forces, which you created in the past based on ignorance, you create karma in the present by daily actions based on attachment and grasping, which are causes and conditions for more suffering in the future. We always create our own life in this way. This is the idea of karma.

Karma becomes the mainstream of our present world because karma, as *samskara,* is the first movement of human beings. That first movement is based on ignorance as the state of being in which one is doomed not to know the truth as it is. As human beings, we are constantly present in the truth, but we are doomed not to know the truth exactly. For example, if I say I am Katagiri, I know who I am, but how much do I really know? It's just a speck of dust. If I say that this is my life, it seems that I know what life is. But how much do I really know about life? I don't know. But even though I don't know, I am already right in the middle of life. We are always right in the middle of the truth, but we don't know it. That situation is really the basic nature of human life, which is called *avidya*.

Avidya doesn't mean we ignore the truth; we want to know, but we are doomed not to know the truth exactly as it is. That is really painful for us. *Avidya* is really pain and affliction; that is called *klesha*. *Klesha* is not exactly ignorance, but it is *avidya* as pain or affliction. Pain or affliction is suffering, that's why Buddha said that human life is characterized by suffering. *Avidya* is not karma, but it's *klesha,* so it's a quality of karma. In other words, it supports and preserves karma. Karma as *samskara* comes from *avidya;* that's why the quality of the first movement of human beings is pain and affliction. Then this movement is the driving force for leaving the source of being to enter the human world. How do you enter? How do you create the human world? How do you create your own life? The movement of *samskara* guides you.

Samskara means to be the together-maker. The basic nature of human activity is to put things together and make something; we are always creating. This energy is *samskara,* putting everything together as the origination of the human world. It is the driving force that leads us to create the human world by accepting human consciousness, and then human existence. Existence is the present situation: we are alive as human beings in the dualistic world, and we act in a certain way.

Karma as *samskara,* formative forces, is unmanifested karma—all the stored actions of everyone's individual life. When the door of that big storage is closed, your life is exactly the same as another person's life. But when the door is opened, by causes and conditions you create or are created by others, *samskara* guides you to enter into the human world. Then, in the human world, you manifest yourself as an individual form of being by actions that are completely different from others' actions. That is karma as *bhava,* being.

But in terms of origination and destruction, a being is neither being nor nonbeing, because nothing exists constantly. Everything is a transient form of being that is constantly becoming. Origination is defined as becoming from nothing to a being; destruction is becoming from a being to a not-being. So, what is a being?

A being is an event in time and space. All beings interconnect with each other in emptiness. Then, according to causes and conditions, something happens and many elements come together to form a being. In terms of origination, *samskara* becomes *bhava.* That is interdependent co-origination, or *pratitya-samutpada.* In Sanskrit, *pratitya* means "dependently," *sam* means "together," and *utpada* is "to originate or occur." So it means "originating dependent on conditions." In terms of destruction, *bhava* becomes *samskara.* All sentient beings return to emptiness and are interconnected in peace and harmony. Then all sentient beings become the next moment of existence and there is change.

From moment to moment your individual life is constantly created anew. So don't accept the idea that there is a certain unchangeable life pattern controlled by something or someone. Buddhism teaches how your life is going through the past, present, and future. Watch your life carefully. In daily living your past life comes up like a jack-in-the-box. *Pop!* You don't feel good, but this is okay. You still have the freedom to make a choice of how to manifest your life now. Then your actions in the present create causes and conditions for your life in the future.

Strictly speaking, karma is at the basis of human life. But it is not inside life; it is not outside life. No matter how long you try to peel the skin, take out the bones, and peek into the marrow, you cannot find something called karma. You cannot find anything at all.

So how can you know karma? We don't know how to know karma, but karma is closely related to the human world through your body and mind. That is the whole body and mind, connected with consciousness, name and form, six sense consciousnesses, contact, feeling, craving, grasping, and being. Through your human body and mind you can know what karma is, what the basis of human existence is. That means stand up in your life, calm your body and mind, and just be present right now, right here. Do zazen, and then you can understand. There is really no other better way, because karma is not something you can fully understand intellectually.

Karma is nothing but energy, the mainspring of creating vitality. If you see this original nature of karma, if you really understand this, that is called freedom. Freedom means that in the next moment you can manifest your life in a new way.

There are two ways of manifesting your life every day: there is an ordinary life and a bodhisattva life. The ordinary type of life is to live in past karma as a cause and delusions as a conditioned element. "Past karma" means that your life extends from the past into the future. You cannot completely understand your life just according to the present. If you really look at your life, you can't say where lots of things come from. They appear outside your effort and carry you in a direction you never expected.

In ordinary life we are always looking at life through our egoistic telescope: judging and evaluating, barking at each other and fighting, always trying to get something for ourselves. This is the ordinary type of karma as cause for an ordinary type of life. In order for this cause to ripen, ordinary living uses the delusion of ignorance as a conditioned element.

But for bodhisattvas there is another type of living. To live the bodhisattva life is to live in vow as a cause and the *paramitas* as a conditioned element. A bodhisattva is the person who vows to help others under all circumstances. In order to make that vow mature, bodhisattva practice has six fundamental principles of human life that are secondary causes to make the primary cause ripen. These are the six *paramitas:* giving, precepts, patience, effort, *samadhi,* and wisdom.

The significance of practicing the six *paramitas* is not how much you do it or how much you accomplish; it is the mind and heart just constantly aiming at the cause of helping others. If you take the best care of one moment, offering yourself to your activity, letting your life touch the ground of existence, and handling the phenomenal world with wisdom and compassion, you turn a new leaf—360 degrees. In the next moment a completely new life appears, and that life helps others.

Turning over a new leaf is called awakening to awareness. If you totally accept your karma and get a taste of it, you can see your life turning a new way. For instance, if I behave in a strange way, you may say, "You are strange." If I reply, "No, I am pretty usual," I will continue to behave in the same way. But if I totally accept it, I can say "Yes!" When I say "Yes!" my life has already turned a new way.

If you look at yourself objectively, you can see many dregs of delusion stirring up muddy water: ignorance, arrogance, craving, hatred, and so on. We should understand how ignorant we are, but we don't stay with it. Whatever we feel, we try to move toward the future, to enhance and develop ourselves. That way, when you realize how ignorant you are, instead of trying to escape ignorance or staying with ignorance and enjoying it or feeling bad, you will naturally want to deepen yourself. We realize how ignorant we are, and in the next moment we try to deepen our life in order to help all sentient beings. That means we can take advantage of the realization of our own ignorance to make our life anew. How? We can make repentance to the Buddha.

When you see your delusion, in the very next moment make repentance. Repentance means to be one with your buddha-nature and make your life anew. This is our practice. Positively, with our own initiative, we have to create the effort to make repentance.

Whoever you are, whatever karma has accumulated in your life, however you feel about your life, just accept it and make repentance to the Buddha. At that time Buddha opens his hands and accepts you. The vast gate of Buddha's compassion is always open to everyone. So accept Buddha's compassion with readiness. Then, through making repentance, you can return with that karma to the source of karma, the source of the repetition of life and death. At that time there is no you and no Buddha. There is just oneness. That is called freedom.

Even though there is lots of karma interrupting your daily living, you can be free from your karmic life anytime, anywhere. From moment to moment, just return to the source of karma, which is called emptiness. Emptiness means that the original nature of human existence is nothing but movement.

The content of emptiness is interdependent co-origination; interdependent co-origination is exactly the teaching of emptiness. Simply speaking, interdependent co-origination is called the rhythm of life. Theoretically we say interdependent co-origination, but empirically it is the rhythm of life. Causes and conditions are working together rhythmically, like the seasons: winter doesn't come right after spring; there is a rhythm, so summer comes after spring—the seasons are never mixed up. That is the rhythm of life on a huge scale, going constantly, beyond your human speculation. It's vast, so you cannot control it. Sometimes we say this is universal life.

When you take a picture of your human existence with your dualistic consciousness, you believe there is a solid being. But it's like a coin turning on the bottom of a string. The functioning of energy leaves something behind, an impression that is left by the spinning coin, and you believe that you see a ball. The ball is a provisional being that seems to be solid, but it isn't. Karma is the same. Karma is nothing but movement, energy, constantly moving in all directions. Karma is directly, closely related to the human world. Vitality is the form of the dualistic world and also the nature of karma. So karma is just like the vitality of life: day by day, moment to moment, you are alive.

We must constantly live by taking the initiative to make our human existence come alive in emptiness. This is our practice. If you do this, repentance simultaneously helps you and also purifies you. Repentance means you can purify yourself. Then, from emptiness a new life comes up. Purifying, helping yourself, helping all sentient beings, you create your own circumstances. Simultaneously, those circumstances help you sustain your effort. If you make repentance like this, you can create your world exactly in a moment.

Turning over a new leaf is exactly connected with the teaching of stillness and dynamism. If you receive the rhythm of life in a passive way it is called fate. In Buddhism we say karma, but plainly speaking it is fate. Fate is sometimes considered as doom, or something wrong or bad. But karma in Buddhism is not something wrong; it is the rhythm of universal life, going constantly, beyond good or bad, right or wrong. If you accept the rhythm of life in a passive way, it is temporarily called fate because we don't understand.

For example, I don't really understand why I am living here in the United States. Also, I don't understand why, when Americans go to Japan, they love Japan. Japan is very small. I love the United States; it's huge! Why am I here? Why do they love Japan? I don't know why.

You don't know why your life is the way it is, so you say it's fate. But you should just quietly accept the broad scale of your life, supported by the past, present, and future, beyond your intellectual understanding. This is total acceptance of your life. Then fate means stillness.

On the other hand, if you receive the huge rhythm of life in a positive way it is called virtuous quality. The foundation of your life is a kind of rich soil. Whatever goes into the rich soil of your life, you have the great capability to digest it and then act. That is dynamism. Dynamism is the richness of your life. It's working constantly so you can always do something, but dynamism must be backed by stillness.

In Buddhist teaching, stillness means emptiness. If you accept emptiness in a passive way, it is called aloneness. That is a very deep sense of aloneness. When you see the bottom of your life, you see emptiness right there. You are standing by yourself, completely left alone in emptiness. It's not something wrong; it's a kind of clue to stand up in a new way. If you accept your aloneness in a positive way, it is called togetherness or creativity. You experience perfect aloneness and simultaneously you see togetherness. That is called awareness or enlightenment.

The depth of the phenomenal world is stillness, but there is dynamism there. When you feel the emptiness of human existence, compassion comes up. You feel your own complete aloneness, then that aloneness is extended to others because you see that all other lives are going in the same way. At that time you really want to do something for others. That is called bodhisattva—the active aspect of Buddha. Bodhisattva and buddha-nature work together. In space it is Buddha; in the time process it is bodhisattva. At the intersection of time and space, a bodhisattva constantly becomes alive from emptiness, and that life helps others.

Through karma you can understand how vast your life is and how you can accumulate virtuous quality in the depth of your life. So stand up in your life, accepting the whole situation. That means total acceptance of your life. It's very hard to accept difficult circumstances in a positive way, but this is your opportunity to act in a new way and create a new life.

Religious practice is stillness in dynamism, dynamism in stillness. Dogen Zenji says practice is just to walk in the mist. Before you realize it, your clothes get wet. Let karma penetrate your clothes, skin, muscle, and bone. Finally you understand what the mist is. Through spiritual practice you develop the great capability to accept the many circumstances of everyday life and digest them. Then you see, "I can change my life!" You can change your life because you accept many things in the broad scale of life. Many things come to you, and you are not what you were. At that time you turn over a new leaf.

33 FREEDOM FROM CAUSATION

Daily life should be just like the water in the Ganges River. The river is huge, and the water is moving very smoothly and quietly. But if you look at your daily life, it's not like water in the Ganges River. It's more like water in a little creek, always making noise, always creating distress and confusion.

We have to find a way to live in the world just like the water in the Ganges River, but it is very difficult. More or less, wherever you may go you will find stress and pressure. There is always pressure among people: stress coming from the self, from others, from family, from society. So you continually try to improve yourself, find a better life, or do something good. Then if you see your life improving, you feel good. But even though you find a better life, it is not peaceful for you because you cannot settle in that life. It isn't really an improvement because you don't feel satisfaction. That's pretty hard. We cannot ignore such a way of life, because this is part of our life. But the important point is: how can we deal with this kind of life? How do we take good care of this kind of life?

In Buddhism there are two ways to take care of human life: according to the law of causation and according to freedom from causation. This is very important.

If you try to take care of your life only according to causation, you are always restless. You cannot find peace. You feel that something is always compelling you to do something, so you are always busy, always irritating yourself to do something more. It's very difficult to deal with this irritation and dissatisfaction because human beings always think in terms of success and failure. If we don't have a completely peaceful life, we become confused and distressed—we don't feel good.

Living in the small world of causation is important because, whatever you do, you have to live according to the rule of causation. But this is not the final goal we have to reach; we also have to live in the big world of freedom from causation.

When I was growing up, my family ran a restaurant. My parents were very busy taking care of business every day, and they had ten kids. I was the youngest, and there were lots of other kids to take care of me, so my parents didn't pay attention to me. There wasn't a comfortable feeling between my parents and me. My brothers and sisters took care of me pretty well, but I always felt pressured by them, so I didn't feel comfortable. Even though I was living with my family, it was nothing but the analytical world of business and brothers and sisters. And when I was ten, my mother became sick, so she was always in bed.

I don't remember any warm relationship, but one thing I remember very well. One day my mother and I had a trip together. We walked to a shrine on top of a hill where we could see the Sea of Japan. My mother was already not in good health, and she couldn't walk very well. She often stopped and sat at the side of the road, bending her knees and resting for a while. Many times she stopped like this—I remember it very well. I played near my mother and kept watching her. I felt good because my mother was there with me. I had never experienced being with her that way.

When we reached the shrine, we sat on a rough bench and watched the sea from the top of the hill. It was a very beautiful scene. We drank a cup of tea and ate a little *umeboshi* cake. I still remember the nice taste of that little cake in the shape of the sour *umeboshi* plum. Nothing special happened—we just sat there, eating that cake—but I felt really comfortable. That memory is very clear for me. Spending the day with my mother, just being present with her. No disturbance, no brothers there, just my mother and I, just living.

This is the full aliveness of life, interconnected with all beings beyond time: beyond past and future or before and after. This is finding a peaceful and harmonious life in the vast expanse of the ocean beyond good or bad, right or wrong, beyond the intellectual world, beyond time and space. It is my mother and I just being present together, taking a walk. That is really nice. You cannot understand it intellectually, because it is completely beyond knowing where that experience came from or who created it. Mother must be just mother as she is, and I must be just I as I am. That's all. That is very wonderful.

It's just like a baby that stops crying when her mother picks her up. The baby immediately feels what human warmth is. That warmth is the full aliveness of life, where everything is interconnected. The mother's life and past life and the baby's past life and future life are interpenetrated. You cannot conceptualize it. There is just the reality of the mother embracing her baby. That's all. At that time the baby stops crying.

Kids today experience lots of pressure coming from themselves, their brothers and sisters, their parents, and their school. But children don't say anything about that. They don't know how to be free from that pressure and discomfort, so they just cry or feel distressed about going to school. That is a signal of their need to become peaceful and harmonious. So sometimes a mother or father should just be present with her or his children: go somewhere, take a walk with them. That's enough. That is living in the vast expanse of the ocean, not the small world of always trying to find a better life. That's when Katagiri as a child becomes just child as I am, and my mother becomes just mother as she is. This is freedom from causation. That's pretty good for us. That experience makes a really great impression. That's why I have a very clear memory of it.

Freedom from causation means oneness of cause and effect. According to the law of causation, if you want to cross a river from one shore to the other shore, there is cause and result. You want to get to the other shore as a result, so you leave where you are as a cause. To do that, you start by taking one step forward. But if you take one step with wholeheartedness, one step is not just one step; one step is simultaneously one hundred steps—the whole area between this shore and the other shore—because when you act with wholeheartedness, cause and effect are absorbed into your activity. At that time cause is not something separate from result and result is not something separate from cause. Cause and effect are one. That is freedom from causation.

Freedom from causation is emptiness. Anytime, anywhere, you can be free from your karmic life, because your karmic life is going on in Buddha's world. That is the reality of one step. To live your life freely, in peace and harmony, all you have to do is wholeheartedly take care of one step in every moment. In that moment you reach the other shore, because one step is not separate from life, it is the full aliveness of life, interconnected with grass, water, your feelings, your body, and many things. In one step there is a peaceful life. This shore, the other shore, and many beings exist, and all are absorbed into that one step. At that time one step becomes just peaceful life.

One step is practice itself. When you practice zazen, the important thing is not seeking a result from zazen. If you seek something from zazen, it's stress and pressure; you're always trying to find something better. Of course it's important to want to improve yourself, but it's not the final goal; it's just the scenery you have to look at on your trip. The most important point is to constantly take the trip. That is wholehearted activity. That is your practice.

We have to live within the law of causation, but we also have to turn the results of causation into eternal possibility. Eternal possibility is life with no limitation, no separation. It's really vast: you cannot see the other shore, you cannot see this shore, you cannot see anything at all. All you have to do is just be present there and move. When your life is present right in the middle of eternal possibility, a wonderful feeling comes up. You feel good. You feel peaceful. You can settle yourself in the self and be peaceful in the great relationship between you and the universe. At that time your life is going smoothly and quietly, just like the water in the Ganges River.

34 ETERNAL POSSIBILITY

Buddhism tells us to see the human world and human life not only according to the teaching of causation but also according to the teaching of impermanence. Having these two teachings creates a very contradictory situation. On one hand, there is the law of causation: if you do something, very naturally you will have its result. But on the other hand, everything is impermanent: there is nothing to grasp in your hand.

You cannot deal with human life only according to causation. You also have to deal with it on the basis of impermanence, because the human world is changing from moment to moment. Impermanence isn't change itself; it is what causes change to be. So it is the basic teaching of existence. You cannot see impermanence with your naked eye, but you can see physical and mental change. Within change you can see that the depth of human life is constantly moving, functioning, working and producing, always supporting your life.

To find a peaceful life, first of all you have to settle yourself in the self and in everyday life. According to the rule of causation, if you do something, you will get a result more or less immediately. So you have to get a taste of that result: good, bad, or neutral. Then in the next moment you have to be free from causation. That means you return whatever feeling you get from your experience into eternal possibility.

For five years I lived with a friend while I attended Komazawa University in Tokyo. My friend was a wonderful person, a beautiful person. Sometimes he was bitter and used rough words, but the basis of his life was compassion. There was continuous compassion there, so he always had many visitors. Every day he was discussing some aspect of Buddhism, talking about human life, and counseling human problems.

One day, after he introduced me to his visitors, he said, "This guy Katagiri always falls asleep when he reads a book in Japanese, but he always wakes up when he reads a book in English." Then he said, "Katagiri has the capability of eternal possibility to improve his English," and after that he had a big laugh.

I accepted what he said as an ironic criticism, but I didn't feel good. I didn't think I was falling asleep whenever I read books in Japanese. When he laughed I felt a little relief, but I didn't understand eternity at that time. I thought of eternity as the end of a time you cannot measure, so I thought he meant there was no way to improve my English, and I didn't feel good. But the eternity I understood was not real eternity, it was just my limited idea of time. I didn't understand that eternal possibility means buddha-nature.

Now I have lived for many years in the United States. In the beginning no one could understand what I said when I gave lectures. But I couldn't escape—I had to give lectures. For one and a half hours everyone sat quietly and listened but no one understood my English. I was very surprised that people came to listen to my lectures even though no one understood them, because it's really ridiculous. But people came anyway, so I couldn't stop. I felt good but also pensive and sad, and sometimes I felt really confused and angry, judging myself on how poor my English is and how stupid I am.

Someone says, "Katagiri, your English is pretty good." But I know this is nothing but a compliment. Or someone says, "Your English is terrible." Well, I know this, but I cannot escape from speaking in English. So when I talk about Buddhism in English there is an immediate result—I get a taste of bitterness, or I feel good, or sometimes neutral.

When something happens, whatever it is that you feel, if you stay with that feeling, your life is limited. Then, from that limitation, you create irritation, confusion, stress, and distress. But to live a peaceful life, you cannot stay with that feeling; you have to return the result you have tasted into eternal possibility. That way bitterness will not find bitterness. So when I get a taste from my feeling, I cannot keep that bitter taste warm in my heart. I have to just stand back and read the *Blue Cliff Record* in English, not in Japanese. I have to just study and learn English.

I didn't feel good then, but now I really appreciate American students because I could return the taste of bitterness to eternal possibility and improve my English. Even though I didn't feel good, all I had to do was constantly spring back and just walk step-by-step toward the future. Yes, I did it, but not only I did it. My effort is just a speck of dust. I had to improve my English not in my own small territory but in the realm of eternal possibility. Then all sentient beings helped me to improve my life.

Don't judge your life just by seeing yourself in your own small territory; accept your life as understood by others, too. Accept your self simultaneously with others, and take care of your life in eternal possibility. Eternal possibility is this very moment. It is where you can digest all living beings: your life, others' lives, trees, birds, and all sentient beings, and produce new creative life energy. That's pretty good for us. Then we feel comfortable and peaceful. This is the peaceful life.

You can experience this in zazen. In zazen many things come up: thoughts, emotions, sometimes anger and hatred. But all you have to do is take care of zazen in eternal possibility. It's completely beyond good or bad, right or wrong, so put aside all kinds of imagination fabricated by your consciousness. Don't attach to thoughts and emotions; just let them return to emptiness. Just be present there and swim in buddha-nature. This is living the bodhisattva vow to help all beings. Then the great energy of the universe supports you and you take one step toward the future with all beings.

A few days ago I saw a news story about a person who died when the bridge he was walking on suddenly broke apart. He fell and died, but someone standing right on the edge of the bridge survived. Why? What's the difference? Is there some reason? If you understand your life just in the present and think about dying on the bridge like this, you get really angry and ask, "Why should only I have to die?" This egoistic way of thinking is very common. It comes from a narrow understanding of human life that makes people arrogant.

There's no reason that can explain why one person died. Maybe the person who died did something wrong in the past. Maybe the person who survived did something good in the past. But it's not necessary to put a certain label on it. Just see the long range of life functioning there. That's a pretty good attitude, without arrogance. Then you can be very humble and modest toward your life.

What is your life? It's very complicated. Your intellect compels you to understand, but there is no perfect answer. All you can do is entrust yourself to the life that is given to you now. Live your own life as it really is. But entrusting yourself to your life doesn't mean just accepting it blindly. It means accepting a profound awareness of something that is greater than the intellectual world. It means accepting it and digesting it through your everyday life.

To digest means to take care of your everyday life by totally accepting that there is something greater than the intellectual world. How do you do this? Through everyday life that is impermanent, you have to actually touch something deep that is eternal. By making your body and mind calm, you can go deeply into the human world and touch your life profoundly. Then you can feel what is eternal, not in an intellectual or philosophical way, but in a practical and realistic way.

You are alive now. Now you can touch your life and feel it. But when you die, the opportunity to touch deeply and profoundly is gone. I always feel this. Now I am explaining Buddha's teaching related to the past, present, and future. But in the future I have to die. I want to scream because there will be nothing left.

In the middle of death there is no sense of I, there is just death. So when I participate in death, I won't know what death is because I am not there—my life is gone and I won't feel anything. Even though I have experienced enlightenment, when I die all the enlightenment that I have experienced will be gone. The Zen center and the people there will be gone from me. So I always think that I want to haunt the Zen center after my death. I want to know how people take care of the Zen center. I always laugh about it and say, "Watch out!" But finally, all I can do is face the fact that I have to die. All I can do now is practice Buddha's teaching day by day.

Life and death occur in a moment. In other words, life and death are nothing but moment. You don't believe that your life is a moment, because in everyday life you always have lots of choices. But if you see death, you taste it immediately. Moment and you come together, creating the momentum energy of time, and you and death become one; you have no choice. Life and death are nothing but momentum energy connected with all sentient beings, without exception. You cannot control that enormous energy; you have to walk alone right in the middle of moment, step-by-step, with an open heart. That's all you can do.

Zen Buddhism focuses on day-to-day life because no matter how long you try to understand life and death intellectually, you will never understand by using only your intellect—you cannot feel how deep your life is. Life is really vast, and you can never get a definite solution. I don't mean you should ignore intellectual understanding. You can take care of your intellect by patting it on the head, calming your body and mind, and letting yourself go deeply into the human world that is beyond the intellectual world. This is our practice. Whatever your intellectual understanding brings you, open your heart enough to digest it again and again, deepen it again and again.

If you look at your life spiritually, with the calm mind of wisdom, I think you can see your life connected with the past and going to the future. You don't know why, but your life is already connected with a past life. If you really look at your present life, don't you think so sometimes? Can't you feel in the depth of your life that your life is going in some way beyond your speculation? Why do you study Buddhism? Why do you practice meditation? You don't know why, because life is really deep and profound. In spiritual life you have to taste that profound human life beyond any intellectual understanding of your present life.

I think the purpose of spiritual life is just to go toward the future with great hope. Your life is not limited only to this life. Your life is going to the future: next life, life after next life, maybe life after next, next life. Maybe your life is going forever. When I say this, then you say that Katagiri believes in reincarnation. Yes, I believe that way, but I don't attach to it. Buddhism has unlimited hope about human life and the human world, so we believe in reincarnation or eternity, but we never attach to it. This is a key point.

If I say "eternity" and you attach to it, you create an "ism." Then there are two views on life: nihilism and eternalism. If you believe that after death there is something that exists forever—a soul that never dies—it is eternalism. If you attach to eternalism, you become mystical; your head is flying around and your life is not rooted on earth. Then you are suffocated to death right in the middle of your dark dream of eternalism. But it doesn't satisfy you, so you look around and try to find something else. You look to nihilism and struggle to find something in nihilism that could satisfy your desire, but the same thing occurs. Whichever you choose, it doesn't hit the mark. Whichever way you go, there is always uneasiness or dissatisfaction. So don't create an "ism" from reincarnation. Buddhism accepts reincarnation but never attaches to it. The most important target you have to aim at is right now, right here.

I have lived in the United States for more than twenty-five years. When I look back over the past twenty-five years of my life, asking myself, "Katagiri, what did you do for twenty-five years?" I say, "Yes, I helped Americans for twenty-five years." But I wonder, how much *can* I help life in America? Or I say, "I have taught Buddha's teaching to Americans for twenty-five years." But I also wonder, how much *have* I taught Buddha's teaching? I don't know.

When I think of my life, I realize there are many things I haven't done yet. In Buddhism it is said that there are eighteen thousand scriptures. Can you read eighteen thousand scriptures in one lifetime? Well, I became a priest at the age of eighteen, but there are many scriptures I still haven't read. My mind says that I want to do it, but practically speaking, I don't do it. In my lifetime I cannot finish all the things I want to do.

No matter how long you live, you cannot satisfy all your desires. Your lifetime is not long enough. So I think you should have a next life. You should practice and study now but leave the unfinished job for your next life. In your next life you will see lots of unfinished jobs too. So carry them to your life after the next life. Then you feel relief. If you try to finish everything in this lifetime, you become nervous, irritated, and uneasy. I don't mean that you can be lazy. Of course you should study Buddhism and practice zazen, because you have to understand the human life that is going on forever, moment after moment, life after life.

To study Buddha's teaching is not just to learn something intellectually or to have particular knowledge of spiritual practice. Spiritual life requires the practice of vow. We vow to taste the truth, to save all beings, to master the teachings, or to accomplish the Buddha Way. We don't understand these vows exactly, but spiritual life requires the practice of living in vow. Your heart and mind must totally accept all sentient beings—past, present, and future—as they truly are. That is called tolerance. Be generous and magnanimous. It isn't a big deal. It's very simple, but it isn't easy, so most people give up.

People don't believe in a long-range life and always see life in the short-range. They want to do something; they want to finish something in this lifetime. Then they become nervous, irritated, and cold. They experience stress and have a nervous breakdown. If you don't take a long-range view of life in the human world, you become crazy. So you have to take care of your life with a long-range hope and just keep going. Every day form a habit of doing small things without expecting any satisfaction of your individual desire. Then your life is just going, in peace and harmony.

Sometimes the more you love spiritual life, the more you create trouble in your family and among your friends. You hate the busy world and want the quiet spiritual life. Then you get out of temper. Most people get out of temper the more they practice meditation. This is not the real spiritual way of life. So even though you don't like your busy life, let's find small things that you can do right in the middle of that busy life. Just light a candle around you, one by one, day by day.

When you take care of your life like this, supreme life is going on, so you can forget the self you believe you are. And then, next, you can go beyond time, because supreme life is connected with the past, present, and future. Very naturally, whether you believe it or not, you go beyond time. You feel a kind of energy between you and the universe. You don't know what it is. It's just like lightning. Sometimes it's slow lightning, but it's lightning. Energy. And then that energy leads you to go ahead constantly. And the more you go, the more you feel that great energy between you and the whole universe. At that time you cannot stop taking care of your life. This is called living in vow.

If you don't understand, please keep your mouth shut and just live with all sentient beings in peace and harmony beyond your intellectual speculation. It's not necessary to think how much that helps people or how many people it helps. All you have to do is be peaceful with people right now, right here, day by day. And then, beyond your expectation, your life will be changed. You can taste something wonderful. You feel relief. At that time a sense of gentleness, generosity, and majesty comes forth from every pore of your body, and it helps all beings.

36   FINDING TIME IN
        BUDDHA'S DHARMA

When you read Buddhist scriptures, you often find expressions of time. Time may be clearly visible or a little hidden, but time is there because the scriptures are saying something about the true nature of your life. Through their words, Buddhist scriptures encourage you to follow the path of spiritual practice and open your eyes to see the truth: your life is changing from moment to moment, together with everything in the universe. When you see the dynamic activity that connects your life with everything that exists you are present in peace and harmony, and very naturally you feel a warm relationship with all beings.

A good example of finding time within the words of a scripture is the short verse, "On Opening the Sutra." For many years people have chanted this verse at Buddhist temples before the teacher gives a dharma talk. Saying this verse helps teacher and students to open their minds and hearts to Buddha's teaching. This verse does not seem to be talking about time, but if we study the words, we find time there. This is the verse:

An unsurpassed, penetrating, and perfect dharma
Is rarely met with, even in a hundred thousand
        million kalpas.

Having it to see and listen to, remember and accept,
I vow to taste the truth of the Tathagata's words.

In the title of this verse, the word *sutra* means "scripture." But there is another meaning for *sutra:* interwoven vertical and horizontal strands or strings. That is human life—the universe is a huge network of interwoven time and space. So sutra is scripture, and it is also human life.

Usually we see only the moments in which we exist day to day, but those moments are within a vast interwoven structure. The word *opening* means to be completely open and see the huge network of time and space very clearly. If you have, even slightly, your own prejudices, desires, and understanding, it is very difficult to open your life. To see the real picture of human life, you have to practice and open yourself. That is called opening the sutra. When you recite this verse, you are vowing to open your eyes and see the truth. The truth you see is called dharma.

Dharma is a Buddhist technical term, a complicated spiritual term with at least three meanings: the principle of existence; all phenomena, visible or invisible; and the teaching. Sometimes we say that dharma is Buddha's compassion, extending everywhere. The huge network of interwoven time and space is exactly the same as dharma. So dharma is a state of being that is always functioning at superspeed, constantly supporting, helping, and nurturing all beings. If you see that state of being, you realize that this is true.

The first line of this verse says that dharma is unsurpassed, penetrating, and perfect. Another word for unsurpassed is *supreme*. If something is supreme there can be nothing more, so dharma is the highest level of being. Next it says that dharma is penetrating, but you can also say profound. Dharma is deep and unfathomable; you cannot touch it. But if you open yourself, open your heart, you can see it and be present there in peace and harmony. Finally it says that dharma is perfect, which means subtle, wondrous, or inconceivable. Dharma is inconceivable— your mind cannot pin down what it is exactly. If you try to explain it objectively, you cannot do it, but you can experience it and know that it is always with you.

In the second line this verse says that dharma is rarely met with, even in a hundred thousand million *kalpas*. *Kalpa* is an expression of time—eternal, boundless, countless time. A hundred thousand million *kalpas* is a long, long time. It is very rare for us to be born as human beings, and very rare for us to have the opportunity to meet, listen to Buddha's teaching, and practice zazen together. But we don't understand how rare it is. Someone who sees a baby about to fall into a lake, and before thinking about it runs to save the baby, has an opportunity to go beyond the ordinary self and meet the dharma. But that kind of opportunity is very rare in daily life, because we are always groping for something in the realm of choices and alternatives. In spiritual life, we have a great opportunity to open ourselves and express ourselves as we really are, prior to the functioning of desire, thought, or speculation. That's why spiritual life is important. So pay attention to zazen! You may not get this opportunity again for a hundred thousand million *kalpas*.

The third line says that dharma is here for us to see

and listen to, remember, and accept. The word *remember* doesn't only mean to remember the talk you are going to hear; it has another meaning. Buddhism sees human life with a long view, which means the present is more or less linked with the past and also the future. The fact that you are interested in your spiritual life is the result of virtuous qualities that you accumulated in the past. You have the opportunity now to remember your original buddha-nature, the real picture of human life, because you knew it in the past. Even though the moment you were born you completely forgot that past life, maybe you can see its dim image through your present life. So listen to Buddha's teaching again and again, because now you have the opportunity to remember it and maintain it for the future.

If you listen to Buddha's teaching, gradually your mind becomes magnanimous. Then, very naturally, a vow comes up. That is the fourth line: I vow to taste the truth of the Tathagata's words. A *tathagata* is a person who is fully enlightened, so the Tathagata's words are Buddha's teaching. Saying this means I vow to open myself and see clearly the network of interwoven time and space that is the unsurpassed, penetrating, and perfect dharma. This vow expresses the total joy and gratitude of realizing how lucky we are to exist as human beings, sharing our life with all beings. It is saying: I am resolved to listen and try to understand the true meaning of Buddha's teaching, and I will try to walk in the deep course of practicing Buddha's teaching forever.

When you chant this verse, remember that you are already living in the dharma because your life is included in the huge network of interwoven time and space. At the intersection of time and space, all beings arise together and exist based on the functioning of interdependent co-origination. According to Buddhism, the whole universe is working dynamically at superspeed, constantly changing, and producing new life from moment to moment.

Scientists try to explain the origin of life, thinking, for example, that it may lie in chemical elements. In Buddhism we say that beings spring from conditions: when the time is ripe and conditions are arranged, something happens. We don't know why the time is ripe, because the time process is too quick for our minds to catch. We don't know why conditions are arranged, because there are many formative forces, both visible and invisible, so it's very complicated. But when time is ripe and conditions are arranged, beings appear as a moment of existence.

When beings appear, why do you happen to exist as the particular being that you are now? You don't know exactly why, but you are a being whose life is already supported by the vast network of time and space. When a particular being arises, it is not just one thing that arises—all beings arise simultaneously. One thing can't arise alone because all life is deeply interconnected and nothing has its own independent existence. So when you as chemical elements arise, then many things happen simultaneously, and trees, birds, sky, and all beings also arise. That is the beginning of the world. You don't believe it, but this is true. When you are born, the whole world is born with you. When you die, the whole world dies with you.

Sometimes you can arrange the conditions of your life by yourself, but not always. There are many conditions that you cannot control because many myriad conditions exist simultaneously. For instance, you try to create good conditions for driving your car, but while you are driving somebody hits your car. What produced that time and arranged those conditions? You don't know. The fact that I exist as Katagiri, the Zen teacher, is completely beyond my intellectual ideas about why I am here, because I am already here, produced by time and conditions.

I can control some conditions in my life, but most I cannot. Sometimes I don't like giving talks. When I look at my English, I hate my English. When my emotions are not peaceful and my body is sick, I don't want to talk. But people say, "Katagiri, you are our teacher. Please come here, sit down, and talk." The time is ripe and conditions are arranged for me to talk. So I sit down.

The moment that exists when time is ripe and conditions are arranged is very important. It is the present moment of *now*. Now is important because the moment that is right here, right now, is eternal, abiding forever. What does eternal mean? It means that, moment after moment, right now appears as all beings; then again: right now; and again: right now. Right now appears forever, that's why *now* is eternal. It means that even though right now appears as an independent moment, this moment is connected to the next moment because it is produced by time and conditions that are handed down from generation to generation, from the past to the present to the future, in a continuous process of interconnected origination. Every moment is a crucial moment because it produces the conditions of the next moment. That is the dynamic reality of the universe we are living in.

The universe can't be seen easily because it's a vast and open space. What you can see is right now, a moment, the present time. But this present is not just the present; it's connected with the whole universe. That is how you can see the universe. If you see this universe, you realize that you are part of a dynamic reality that is constantly changing according to the conditions of every moment. Then you understand why your human life is important. It is important because, if you take care of this *right now* with wholeheartedness, you create good conditions for the next *right now*. That's why Buddhist teachers always tell you to take good care of your life. So do your best to take care of every moment with a warm heart, because your life is simultaneously the life of all beings.

When you study Buddha's teaching, carefully and deeply investigate this very moment, penetrating the present time with a clear mind and seeing human life with deep insight. This is our important practice. That's why we do zazen. Zazen means the sitting meditation we do and simultaneously it means *samadhi*. In *samadhi* your mind and body extend into every inch of the universe because you become one with the universe. That is to open the sutra, taste the truth of Buddha's teaching, and see the real picture of human life.

Buddha's teaching is really vast and magnificent. So even if you don't understand the meaning exactly, you shouldn't stop trying. You always have an opportunity to see Buddha's teaching because no one, nothing, is outside of Buddha's teaching. Buddha constantly extends his compassion to every inch of the universe. Buddha's hands and heart support everything and everyone, whoever they are, wherever they may go. If you open yourself completely, it hits your heart. Then you appreciate that dharma, Buddha's compassion, the ultimate nature of existence, or whatever words you use, is always helping and supporting your life.

When you realize how the universe is, you say that it is Buddha's vow. The term *Buddha's vow* is a way of saying that the universe is working constantly, nurturing all beings, beyond our intellectual speculation. Buddha's vow is like a mother's existence for her baby. A baby doesn't know what a mother is. But whether or not the baby is conscious of it, the baby is present in peace and harmony because there is a mother. Even when a mother is not touching her baby, she is always holding the baby in her warm hands and heart, wherever she is, whatever she does. That's why the baby grows.

Buddha's vow is just like springwater that constantly comes up in a well. We are supported by the energy of that water coming up. Because of Buddha's vow we can live, we can walk. You and I are already walking together on the path of the Buddha Way, completely supported by Buddha's warm hands. When we realize the original nature of the universe, we see that all beings are living and walking together, hand in hand, in peace and harmony, without making any discrimination. If there is no discrimination, nothing has an independent existence, and there is nothing particular we can depend on other than Buddha's vow. So let's walk together, supported by Buddha's warm hands, in the universe that is Buddha's vow.

SELECTED BIBLIOGRAPHY

Bielefeldt, Carl. *Dōgen's Manuals of Zen Meditation*. Berkeley and Los Angeles: University of California Press, 1988.

Cleary, Thomas. *Rational Zen: The Mind of Dōgen Zenji*. Boston: Shambhala Publications, 1992.

———, trans. *Shōbōgenzō: Zen Essays by Dōgen*. Honolulu: University of Hawaii Press, 1986.

Cook, Francis Dojun. *How to Raise an Ox: Zen Practice as Taught in Zen Master Dogen's "Shobogenzo."* Los Angeles: Center Publications, 1978. Reprint, Somerville, Mass.: Wisdom Publications, 2002.

Cook, Francis H. *Sounds of Valley Streams: Enlightenment in Dōgen's Zen; Translations of Nine Essays from "Shōbōgenzō."* Albany: State University of New York Press, 1989.

Dogen. *Shōbōgenzō: Treasury of the Eye of the True Dharma*. Online translations by the Soto Zen Text Project. Stanford Center for Buddhist Studies, in progress. www.stanford.edu/group/scbs/sztp3/.

Dōgen, and Kōshō Uchiyama. *Refining Your Life: From the Zen Kitchen to Enlightenment*. Translated by Thomas Wright. New York: Weatherhill, 1983. Reissued as *How to Cook Your Life*. Boston: Shambhala Publications, 2005.

Kennett, Jiyu. *Selling Water by the River: A Manual of Zen Training*. New York: Pantheon Books, 1972. Reissued as *Zen Is Eternal Life*. 4th ed. Mount Shasta, Calif.: Shasta Abbey Press, 2000.

Kim, Hee-jin. *Dōgen Kigen: Mystical Realist*. 3rd rev. ed. Somerville, Mass.: Wisdom Publications, 2004.

Nishijima, Gudo, and Chodo Cross, trans. *Master Dōgen's "Shōbōgenzō," Books 1-4*. London: Windbell Publications, 1994.

Tanahashi, Kazuaki, ed. *Moon in a Dewdrop: Writings of Zen Master Dōgen*. San Francisco: North Point Press, 1985.

Waddell, Norman, and Masao Abe, trans. *The Heart of Dōgen's "Shōbōgenzō."* Albany: State University of New York Press, 2002.

Yokoi, Yūhō, with Daizen Victoria. *Zen Master Dōgen: An Introduction with Selected Writings*. New York: Weatherhill, 1976.

INDEX

ABOUT THE AUTHOR

Dainin Katagiri was a central figure in the transmission of Zen Buddhism to America. He was born in Osaka, Japan, in 1928 and was ordained by Daicho Hayashi Roshi at Taizoin temple in Fukui when he was eighteen. He trained at Eiheiji monastery for three years under the guidance of Eko Hashimoto Roshi and later attended Komazawa University, completing a master's degree in Buddhist studies.

Katagiri Roshi came to the United States in 1963, when he was called to serve at the Zenshuji Soto Zen Mission in Los Angeles. Shortly after that he transferred to Sokoji Soto Zen Mission in San Francisco, but he soon became affiliated with American Zen at the rapidly grow-ing San Francisco Zen Center, where he assisted Shunryu Suzuki Roshi until Suzuki Roshi's death in 1971.

He was then invited to form a new Zen center in the American Midwest, and in 1972 he moved to Minneapo-lis to become the first abbot of the Minnesota Zen Medi-tation Center. There he oversaw the development of the city center, Ganshoji, as well as Hokyoji Zen Monastery, built in the quiet hills of southeastern Minnesota.

When Katagiri Roshi died in 1990, he left a legacy of recorded teachings, twelve dharma heirs, and many devoted students. Many who studied with him have since become Zen teachers, and there are now several Zen centers in the Katagiri Roshi lineage.

His first book, *Returning to Silence*, was published by Shambhala in 1988, followed by *You Have to Say Something* in 1998.

BOOKS BY DAININ KATAGIRI

Returning to Silence: Zen Practice in Daily Life

Based on Katagiri Roshi's talks to his American students, *Returning to Silence* contains the basic teachings of the Buddha, with special emphasis on meditation and on the meaning of faith. It also offers a commentary to "The Bodhisattva's Four Methods of Guidance" from Dogen Zenji's *Shobogenzo,* which explores in depth the appropriate actions of those who guide others in the practice of the Buddha Way. Throughout these pages, Katagiri Roshi energetically brings to life the message that "Buddha is your daily life."

You Have to Say Something: Manifesting Zen Insight

In *You Have to Say Something,* selections from Katagiri Roshi's talks have been collected and edited to address a key theme of his teachings: how to bring Zen insight to bear on our everyday experience.